INSTRUCTIONS

TO THE

SURVEYORS GENERAL OF PUBLIC LANDS

OF

THE UNITED STATES,

FOR THOSE

SURVEYING DISTRICTS ESTABLISHED IN AND SINCE THE YEAR 1850;

CONTAINING, ALSO,

A MANUAL OF INSTRUCTIONS

TO

REGULATE THE FIELD OPERATIONS OF DEPUTY SURVEYORS.

ILLUSTRATED BY DIAGRAMS.

PRESCRIBED, ACCORDING TO LAW, BY THE PRINCIPAL CLERK OF SURVEYS, PURSUANT TO ORDER OF THE COMMISSIONER OF THE GENERAL LAND OFFICE.

WASHINGTON:
GOVERNMENT PRINTING OFFICE.
1871.

TO THE SURVEYORS GENERAL

OF

PUBLIC LANDS OF THE UNITED STATES

FOR THE

SURVEYING DISTRICTS ESTABLISHED IN AND SINCE THE YEAR 1850.

By the direction of the Commissioner of the General Land Office, the accompanying instructions are prescribed for your official government, including a Manual of Instructions to regulate the field operations of your deputy surveyors. The latter is a revision of the Manual of Surveying Instructions prepared for Oregon in 1851, (the edition of which is now exhausted,) and presents, in some respects, more copious illustrations, both in the specimen field notes and in the diagrams, than could be furnished amid the pressure of the exigency under which the former had to be prepared. It will be observed that, in the former edition, the township and section lines south of the base are made to start therefrom, and close on the first standard parallel south; whereas, under the present instructions, such lines are made to start from the first standard parallel south, and to close to the north on the base; and thus there will be closing corners and starting corners, both on the base and standard lines. Such modification is introduced for the sake of entire uniformity of method in new fields of survey, and will not, of course, affect any past operations under the original instructions.

The starting corners on the base line and on the standards will, of course, be common to two townships or to two sections lying on and north of such lines; and the closing corners on such lines, from the south, should be carefully connected with the former by measurements to be noted in the field book.

Where STONE can be had to perpetuate corner boundaries, such, for obvious reasons, should always be preferred for that purpose, and the dimensions of the stone, as herein prescribed, (on page 9,) are to be regarded as the *minimum size;* but in localities where it is found practicable to obtain a stone of *increased dimensions*, it is always desirable to do so, particularly for TOWNSHIP CORNERS, and especially for those on base, meridian, and standard lines; and to such purport the deputy surveyor is to be especially instructed.

Prior to entering upon duty, the deputy surveyor is to make himself thoroughly acquainted with the official requirements in regard to field operations in all the details herein set forth, and to be apprised of the weighty moral and legal responsibilities under which he will act.

Unfaithfulness in the execution of the public surveys will be detected by special examinations of the work to be made for that purpose, and, when detected, will immediately subject the delinquent deputy and his bondsmen to be sued by the district attorney of the United States, at the instance of the proper surveyor general—the institution of which suit will act at once as a lien upon any property owned by him or them at that time; and such delinquency, moreover, is an offense punishable by the statute, with all the pains and penalties of perjury, (see act of 1846, quoted on pages 19 and 20 hereof,) and will of necessity debar the offending deputy from future employment in like capacity. Hence, in the execution of contracts for surveying public lands, there is every incentive to fidelity that can address itself either to the moral sense or to motives of private interest.

By order of the Commissioner:

JOHN M. MOORE,
Principal Clerk of Surveys.

GENERAL LAND OFFICE,
February 22, 1855.

TABLE OF CONTENTS.

	Page.
System of rectangular surveying; range, township, and section lines; mode of numbering townships and sections; standard parallels	7, 8
Of measurements, chaining, and marking; tally pins; process of chaining	8, 9
Marking lines; of trial or random lines	9
Insuperable objects on line; witness points; marking irons	9, 10
Establishing corner boundaries; at what points for township, section, quarter section, and meander corners, respectively	10, 11
Manner of establishing corners by means of posts	11, 12
Notching corner posts	12
Bearing trees; how many at the different corners, and how to be marked	12
Stones for corner boundaries; minimum size; marking same	13
Mounds around posts, of earth or stone; how to be constructed and conditioned	13, 14
Mound memorials; witness mounds to corners	14
Double corners only on base and standard parallels	14, 15
Meandering navigable streams, lakes, and deep ponds	15–17
Field books for deputy surveyors	17, 18
Summary of objects and data to be noted in field books	18, 19
Swamp lands granted to the State by act of 28th September, 1850; their outlines to be specially noted by the deputy surveyor	19, 20
Noting of settlers' claims in Oregon, Washington, and New Mexico	20
Affidavits to field notes, and provisions of act of 8th August, 1846, respecting the same; pains and penalties which attach to false surveys	20
Forms of official oaths, prior to entering upon duty, for a deputy and his assistants	21
Exteriors or township lines, and limitations within which they must close	21, 22
Method of subdividing	22–24
Limitations within which section and meander lines must close	24
Of Diagram A, showing a body of township exteriors	24
Of Diagram B, showing the subdivision of a township into sections	24
Of Diagram C, illustrating the mode of making mound, stake, and stone corners	24
Subdivisions of fractional sections into forty-acre lots are to be made by the surveyor general on the township plats, and to be designated by special numbers, where they cannot be described as quarter-quarters	24, 25
Township plats to be prepared by the surveyor general in *triplicate*	25
Township plats to be furnished to the General Land Office and to the district land offices; details to be shown thereon, respectively	25
"Descriptive notes," showing the quality of soil and kind of timber found on the surveyed lines in each township, and describing each corner boundary, are to accompany the plat of the same, to be furnished by the surveyor general to the district land office	25
The original field books of surveys, bearing the written approval of the surveyor general, to be retained in his office	25
Certified transcripts of field books to be furnished to General Land Office	25
Meander corners to be numbered on township plats	25
Variation of the needle, and mode of ascertaining the same	26
Specimen field notes A and B—the former of the exterior lines of a township, and the latter of the subdivision of the same—constitute a separate series of pages, from 1 to 53, inclusive; and they are preceded by an INDEX referring the township, section, closing, and meander lines, as shown on Diagram B, to their corresponding pages in the notes A and B	32–68
The "General Description" of the character of public land in the township follows the subdivisional notes, with a "list of names" of assistants, and the mode of authenticating the survey, under the provisions of the act of 8th August, 1846, and form for certifying copies of field notes to be transmitted to the General Land Office	68–70
Conclusion. "Table showing the difference of latitude and departure in running 80 chains, at any course from 1 to 60 minutes"	70

SYSTEM
OF
RECTANGULAR SURVEYING.

1. The public lands of the United States are ordinarily surveyed into rectangular tracts, bounded by lines conforming to the cardinal points.

2. The public lands are laid off, in the first place, into bodies of land of six miles square, called *townships*, containing as near as may be 23,040 acres. The townships are subdivided into thirty-six tracts, called *sections*, of a mile square, each containing as near as may be 640 acres. Any number or series of contiguous townships, situate north or south of each other, constitute a *range*.

The law requires that the lines of the public surveys shall be governed by the true meridian, and that the townships shall be *six miles square*—two things involving in connection a mathematical impossibility—for, strictly to conform to the meridian, necessarily throws the township out of square, by reason of the convergency of meridians, and hence, by adhering to the true meridian, results the necessity of departing from the strict requirements of law, as respects the precise area of townships and the subdivisional parts thereof, the township assuming something of a trapezoidal form, which inequality develops itself more and more as such, the higher the latitude of the surveys. It is doubtless in view of these circumstances that the law provides (see section 2 of the act of May 18, 1796) that the sections of a mile square shall contain the quantity of 640 acres, *as nearly as may be;* and, moreover, provides (see section 3 of the act of 10th May, 1800) in the following words: "And in all cases where the exterior lines of the townships, thus to be subdivided into sections or half sections, shall exceed, or shall not extend six miles, the excess or deficiency shall be specially noted, and added to or deducted from the western or northern ranges of sections or half sections in such township, according as the error may be in running the lines from east to west, or from south to north; the sections and half sections bounded on the northern and western lines of such townships shall be sold as containing only the quantity expressed in the returns and plats, respectively, and all others as containing the complete legal quantity."

The accompanying diagram, marked A, will serve to illustrate the method of running out the exterior lines of townships, as well on the *north* as on the *south* side of the base line; and the order and mode of subdividing townships will be found illustrated in the accompanying specimen field-notes, conforming with the township diagram B. The method here presented is designed to insure as full a compliance with all the requirements, meaning, and intent of the surveying laws as, it is believed, is practicable.

The section lines are surveyed from *south* to north on true meridians, and from *east* to west, in order to throw the excesses or deficiencies in measurements on the north and west sides of the township, as required by law.

3. The townships are to bear numbers in respect to the base line either

north or south of it; and the tiers of townships, called "ranges," will bear numbers in respect to the meridian line according to their relative position to it, either on the east or west.

4. The thirty-six sections into which a township is subdivided are numbered, commencing with number *one* at the *northeast* angle of the township, and proceeding west to number six, and thence proceeding east to number twelve, and so on, alternately, until the number thirty-six in the southeast angle.

5. STANDARD PARALLELS (usually called correction lines) are established at stated intervals to provide for or counteract the error that otherwise would result from the convergency of meridians, and also to arrest error arising from inaccuracies in measurements on meridian lines, which, however, must ever be studiously avoided. On the *north* of the principal base line it is proposed to have these standards run at distances of every *four* townships, or twenty-four miles, and on the *south* of the principal base, at distances of every *five* townships, or thirty miles.

OF MEASUREMENTS, CHAINING, AND MARKING.

1. Where uniformity in the variation of the needle is not found, the public surveys must be made with an instrument operating independently of the magnetic needle. Burt's *improved solar compass*, or other instrument of equal utility, must be used of necessity in such cases; and it is deemed best that such instrument should be used under all circumstances. Where the needle can be relied on, however, the ordinary compass may be used in subdividing and meandering.

2. The township lines, and the subdivision lines, will usually be measured by a two-pole chain of thirty-three feet in length, consisting of fifty links, and each link being seven inches and ninety-two hundredths of an inch long. On uniform and level ground, however, the four-pole chain may be used. Your measurements will, however, always be represented according to the four-pole chain of one hundred links. The deputy surveyor must also have with him a measure of the standard chain, wherewith to compare and adjust the chain in use, from day to day, with punctuality and carefulness; and must return such standard chain to the surveyor general's office for examination when his work is completed.

OF TALLY PINS.

3. You will use eleven tally pins made of steel, not exceeding fourteen inches in length, weighty enough toward the point to make them drop perpendicularly, and having a ring at the top, in which is to be fixed a piece of red cloth, or something else of conspicuous color, to make them readily seen when stuck in the ground.

PROCESS OF CHAINING.

4. In measuring lines with a two-pole chain, every *five* chains are called "a *tally*," because at that distance the last of the ten tally pins with which the forward chainman set out will have been stuck. He then cries "tally;" which cry is repeated by the other chainman, and each registers the distance by slipping a thimble, button, or ring of leather, or something of the kind, on a belt worn for that purpose, or by some other convenient method. The hind chainman then comes up,

and having counted in the presence of his fellow the tally pins which he has taken up, so that both may be assured that none of the pins have been lost, he then takes the forward end of the chain, and proceeds to set the pins. Thus the chainmen alternately change places, each setting the pins that he has taken up, so that one is forward in all the odd, and the other in all the even tallies. Such procedure, it is believed, tends to insure accuracy in measurement, facilitates the recollection of the distances to objects on the line, and renders a mis-tally almost impossible.

LEVELING THE CHAIN AND PLUMBING THE PINS.

5. The length of every line you run is to be ascertained by precise horizontal measurement, as nearly approximating to an air line as is possible in practice on the earth's surface. This all-important object can only be attained by a rigid adherence to the three following observances:

1. Ever keeping the chain *stretched* to its utmost degree of tension on even ground.

2. On uneven ground, keeping the chain not only stretched as aforesaid, but horizontally *leveled*. And when ascending and descending steep ground, hills, or mountains, the chain will have to be *shortened* to one-half its length, (and sometimes more,) in order accurately to obtain the true horizontal measure.

3. The careful plumbing of the tally pins, so as to attain precisely *the spot* where they should be stuck. The more uneven the surface, the greater the caution needed to set the pins.

MARKING LINES.

6. All lines on which are to be established the legal corner boundaries are to be marked after this method, viz: Those trees which may intercept your line must have two chops or notches cut on each side of them without any other marks whatever. These are called "*sight trees*," "*line trees*," or "*station trees*."

A sufficient number of other trees standing nearest to your line, on either side of it, are to be *blazed* on two sides diagonally, or quartering toward the line, in order to render the line conspicuous, and readily to be traced, the blazes to be opposite each other, coinciding in direction with the line where the trees stand very near it, and to approach nearer each other the further the line passes from the blazed trees. Due care must ever be taken to have the lines so well marked as to be readily followed.

ON TRIAL, OR RANDOM LINES,

the trees are not to be blazed, unless occasionally, from indispensable necessity, and then it must be done so guardedly as to prevent the possibility of confounding the marks of the trial line with the *true*. But bushes and limbs of trees may be lopped, and *stakes set* on the trial, or random line, at every *ten* chains, to enable the surveyor on his return to follow and correct the trial line, and establish therefrom the *true line*. To prevent confusion, the temporary stakes set on the trial, or random lines, must be *pulled up* when the surveyor returns to establish the true line.

INSUPERABLE OBJECTS ON LINE—WITNESS POINTS.

7. Under circumstances where your course is obstructed by impassable obstacles, such as ponds, swamps, marshes, lakes, rivers, creeks, &c., you will prolong the line across such obstacles by taking the necessary

right angle offsets; or, if such be inconvenient, by a traverse or trigonometrical operation, until you regain the line on the opposite side. And in case a north and south, or a true east and west, line is regained in advance of any such obstacle, you will prolong and mark the line back to the obstacle so passed, and state all the particulars in relation thereto in your field book. And at the intersection of lines with both margins of impassable obstacles, you will establish a *witness point*, (for the purpose of perpetuating the intersections therewith,) by setting a post, and giving in your field book the course and distance therefrom to two trees on opposite sides of the line, each of which trees you will mark with a blaze and notch facing the post; but on the margins of navigable water courses, or navigable lakes, you will mark the trees with the proper number of the fractional section, township, and range.

☞ The best marking tools adapted to the purpose must be provided for marking neatly and *distinctly* all the letters and figures required to be made at corners; and the deputy is to have always at hand the necessary implements for keeping his marking irons in order; for which purpose a rat-tail file and a small whetstone will be found indispensable.

ESTABLISHING CORNER BOUNDARIES.

To procure the faithful execution of this portion of a surveyor's duty is a matter of the utmost importance. After a true coursing, and most exact measurements, the corner boundary is the consummation of the work, for which all the previous pains and expenditures have been incurred. If, therefore, the corner boundary be not perpetuated in a permanent and workmanlike manner the *great aim* of the surveying service will not have been attained. A boundary corner, in a timbered country, is to be *a tree*, if one be found at the precise spot; and if not, a *post* is to be planted thereat; and the position of the corner post is to be indicated by trees adjacent, the angular bearings and distances of which from the corner are facts to be ascertained and registered in your field-book. (See article, "Bearing trees.")

In a region where stone abounds the corner boundary will be a small *monument of stones* alongside of a single marked stone for a township corner, and a single stone for all other corners.

In a region where timber is not near, and stone not found, the corner will be a *mound of earth*, of prescribed size, varying to suit the case.

The following are the different points for perpetuating corners, viz:
1. For township boundaries, at intervals of every six miles.
2. For section boundaries, at intervals of every mile, or 80 chains.
3. For quarter section boundaries, at intervals of every half mile, or 40 chains. Exceptions, however, occur on east and west lines, as explained hereafter.

[The half-quarter section boundary is not marked in the field, but is regarded by the law as a point intermediate between the half mile or quarter section corners. See act of 24th April, 1820, entitled "An act making further provision for the sale of the public lands," which act refers to the act of Congress passed on the 11th of February, 1805, entitled "An act concerning the mode of surveying the public lands of the United States," for the manner of ascertaining the corners and contents of half-quarter sections.]*

---

* The subdivision of the half-quarter section into quarter-quarter sections is authorized by "An act supplementary to the several laws for the sale of the public lands," approved April 5, 1832.

4. MEANDER CORNER POSTS are planted at all those points where the township or section lines intersect the banks of such rivers, bayous, lakes, or islands, as are by law directed to be meandered.

The courses and distances on meandered navigable streams govern the calculations wherefrom are ascertained the true areas of the tracts of land (sections, quarter sections, &c.) known to the law as *fractional*, and binding on such streams.

MANNER OF ESTABLISHING CORNERS BY MEANS OF POSTS.

Township, sectional, or mile corners, and quarter sectional or half mile corners, will be perpetuated by planting a post at the place of the corner, to be formed of the most durable wood of the forest at hand.

The posts must be set in the earth by digging a hole to admit them *two feet* deep, and must be very securely rammed in with earth, and also with stone, if any be found at hand. The portion of the post which protrudes above the earth must be *squared* off sufficiently smooth to admit of receiving the marks thereon, to be made with appropriate marking irons, indicating what it stands for. Thus the sides of *township corner posts* should square at least *four* inches, (the post itself being *five* inches in diameter,) and must protrude *two feet* at least, above the ground; the sides of *section corner posts* must square at least *three inches*, (the post itself being *four* inches in diameter,) and protrude *two feet* from the ground; and the *quarter section corner posts* and *meander corner posts* must be *three* inches *wide*, presenting *flattened* surfaces, and protruding *two* feet from the ground.

Where a township post is a corner common to *four* townships, it is to be set in the earth *diagonally*, thus:

$$\begin{array}{c} N \\ W \diamond E \\ S \end{array}$$

On each surface of the post is to be marked the number of the particular township, and its range, which it *faces*. Thus, if the post be a common boundary to four townships, say *one* and *two*, south of the base line, of range *one*, west of the meridian; also, to townships *one* and *two*, south of the base line, of range *two*, west of the meridian, it is to be marked thus:

From N. to E. $\begin{Bmatrix} R. & 1 \text{ W.} \\ T. & 1 \text{ S.} \\ S. & 31 \end{Bmatrix}$ from E. to S. $\begin{Bmatrix} 1 \text{ W.} \\ 2 \text{ S.} \\ 6 \end{Bmatrix}$

From N. to W. $\begin{Bmatrix} 2 \text{ W.} \\ 1 \text{ S.} \\ 36 \end{Bmatrix}$ from W. to S. $\begin{Bmatrix} 2 \text{ W.} \\ 2 \text{ S.} \\ 1 \end{Bmatrix}$

These marks are not only to be distinctly but *neatly* cut into the wood, at least the eighth of an inch deep; and to make them yet more *conspicuous* to the eye of the *anxious explorer, the deputy must apply* to all of them a *streak* of *red chalk*.

Section or mile posts, being corners of sections, and where such are common to *four* sections, are to be set *diagonally* in the earth, (in the manner provided for township corner posts;) and on each side of the squared surfaces (made smooth, as aforesaid, to receive the marks) is to be marked the appropriate *number* of the particular one of the *four sections*, respectively, which such side *faces;* also, on one side thereof are to be *marked* the numbers of its *township* and *range;* and to make such marks yet more *conspicuous*, in manner aforesaid, a streak of *red chalk* is to be applied.

In every township, subdivided into thirty-six sections, there are twenty-five interior section corners, each of which will be *common to four* sections.

A quarter section, or half-mile post, is to have no other mark on it than ¼ S., to indicate what it stands for.

NOTCHING CORNER POSTS.

Township corner posts, common to four townships, are to be notched with *six* notches on each of the four angles of the squared part set to the cardinal points.

All mile posts *on township lines* must have as many notches on them, on two opposite *angles* thereof, as they are miles distant from the township corners, respectively. Each of the posts at the corners of sections in the *interior* of a township must indicate, by a number of notches on each of its four corners directed to the cardinal points, the corresponding number of miles that it stands from the *outlines* of the township. The four sides of the post will indicate the number of the section they respectively *face*. Should a tree be found at the place of any corner, it will be marked and notched as aforesaid, and answer for the corner in lieu of a post, the kind of tree and its diameter being given in the field notes.

BEARING TREES.

The position of all corner posts, or corner trees, of whatever description, that may be established, is to be evidenced in the following manner, viz: From such post or tree the courses must be taken and the distances measured to two or more adjacent trees in opposite directions, as nearly as may be, and these are called "bearing trees." Such are to be distinguished by a large *smooth blaze*, with a *notch* at its lower end, facing the corner, and in the blaze is to be marked the number of the *range, township*, and *section ;* but at quarter-section corners nothing but ¼ S. need be marked. The letters B. T. (bearing tree) are also to be marked upon a smaller blaze directly under the large one, and as near the ground as practicable.

At all township corners, and at all section corners, on range or township lines, *four* bearing trees are to be marked in this manner, one in each of the adjoining sections.

At interior section corners *four* trees, one to stand within each of the four sections to which such corner is common, are to be marked in manner aforesaid, if such be found.

A tree supplying the place of a corner post is to be marked in the manner directed for posts, but if such tree should be a beech, or other *smooth bark* tree, the marks may be made on the *bark* and the tree notched.

From quarter section and meander corners two bearing trees are to be marked, one within each of the adjoining sections.

Where the requisite number of "bearing trees" is not to be found at convenient and suitable distances, such as are found are to be marked as herein directed ; but in all such cases of deficiency in the number of bearing trees, (unless, indeed, the boundary itself be *a tree,*) a *quadrangular trench*, with sides of *five* feet, and with the angles to the cardinal points, must be spaded up outside the corner, as a center, and the earth carefully thrown on the inside, so as to form a range of earth, which will become covered with grass, and present a small square elevation, which in after-time will serve to mark unmistakably the spot of the corner.

CORNER STONES.

Where it is deemed best to use STONES for boundaries, in lieu of posts, you may, at *any* corner, insert endwise into the ground, to the depth of 7 or 8 inches, a stone, the number of cubic inches in which shall not be less than the number contained in a stone 14 inches long, 12 inches wide, and 3 inches thick—equal to 504 cubic inches—the edges of which must be set north and south, on north and south lines, and east and west, on east and west lines; the dimensions of each stone to be given in the field notes at the time of establishing the corner. The kind of stone should also be stated.

MARKING CORNER STONES.

Stones at township corners, common to four townships, must have *six* notches, cut with a pick or chisel on each edge or side toward the cardinal points; and where used as section corners on the range and township lines, or as section corners in the interior of a township, they will also be notched, to correspond with the directions given for notching posts similarly situated.

Posts or stones at township corners on the base and standard lines, and which are common to two townships on the north side thereof, will have *six* notches on each of the *west, north,* and *east* sides or edges; and where such stones or posts are set for corners to two townships *south* of the base or standard, *six* notches will be cut on each of the west, *south,* and east sides or edges.

Stones, when used for quarter section corners, will have ¼ cut on them —on the west side on north and south lines, and on the north side on east and west lines.

MOUNDS.

Whenever bearing trees are not found, mounds of earth, or stone, are to be raised *around posts* on which the corners are to be marked in the manner aforesaid. Wherever a mound of earth is adopted, the same will present a conical shape; but at its base, on the earth's surface, a *quadrangular trench* will be dug; by the "trench" (here meant) is to be understood a *spade deep* of earth thrown up from the four sides of the line, *outside* the trench, so as to form a *continuous elevation along its outer edge*. In mounds of earth, common to *four* townships or to *four* sections, they will present the *angles* of the quadrangular trench (*diagonally*) towards the cardinal points. In mounds common only to *two* townships or *two* sections, the *sides* of the quadrangular trench will *face* the cardinal points. The sides of the quadrangular trench at the base of a township mound are to be *six* feet, the height of mound *three* feet.

At section, quarter section, and meander corners, the sides of the quadrangular trench at base of mounds are to be *five* feet, and the conical height *two and a half feet*.

Prior to piling up the earth to construct a mound, there is to be dug a spadeful or two of earth from the corner boundary point, and in the cavity so formed is to be deposited a *marked stone*, or a portion of *charcoal*, (the quantity whereof is to be noted in the field book;) or in lieu of charcoal or marked stone, a *charred stake* is to be driven twelve inches down into such center point: either of those will be a *witness* for the future, and whichever is adopted, the fact is to be noted in the field book.

When mounds are formed of *earth*, the spot from which the earth is taken is called the "*pit*," the center of which ought to be, wherever practicable, at a uniform distance and in a uniform direction from the center of the mound. There is to be a "pit" on *each* side of every mound, distant eighteen inches outside of the trench. The trench may be expected hereafter to be covered by tufts of grass, and thus to indicate the place of the mound, when the mound itself may have become obliterated by time or accident.

At meander corners the "pit" is to be directly on the line, *eight links* further from the water than the mound. Wherever necessity is found for deviating from these rules in respect to the "pits," the course and distance to each is to be stated in the field books.

Perpetuity in the mound is a great desideratum. In forming it with light alluvial soil the surveyor may find it necessary to make due allowance for the future settling of the earth, and thus making the mound more elevated than would be necessary in a more compact and tenacious soil, and increasing the base of it. In so doing, the relative proportions between the township mound and other mounds is to be preserved as nearly as may be.

The earth is to be pressed down with the shovel during the process of piling it up. Mounds are to be *covered* with sod, grass side up, where sod is to be had; but, in forming a mound, *sod* is NEVER to be *wrought up* with the earth, because sod decays, and in the process of decomposing it will cause the mound to become porous, and therefore liable to premature destruction.

POSTS IN MOUNDS

must show above the top of the mound ten or twelve inches, and be notched and marked precisely as they would be for the same corner without the mound.

MOUND MEMORIALS.

Besides the *charcoal*, marked *stone*, or *charred stake*, one or the other of which must be lodged in the earth at the point of the corner, the deputy surveyor is recommended to plant *midway* between each pit and the trench, seeds of some tree, (those of fruit trees adapted to the climate being always to be preferred,) so that, in course of time, should such take root, a small clump of trees may possibly hereafter note the place of the corner. The facts of planting such seed, and the kind thereof, are matters to be truthfully noted in the field-book.

WITNESS MOUNDS TO TOWNSHIP OR SECTION CORNERS.

If a township or section corner, in a situation where bearing or witness trees are not found within a reasonable distance therefrom, shall fall within a ravine, or in any other situation where the nature of the ground, or the circumstances of its locality, shall be such as may prevent, or prove unfavorable to, the erection of a mound, you will perpetuate such corner by selecting in the immediate vicinity thereof a suitable plot of ground as a site for a bearing or *witness mound*, and erect thereon a mound of earth in the same manner and conditioned in every respect, with *charcoal, stone*, or *charred stake* deposited beneath, as before directed; and measure and state in your field-book the distance and course from the position of the true corner of the bearing or witness mound so placed and erected.

DOUBLE CORNERS.

Such corners are to be nowhere except on the base and standard lines, whereon are to appear both the corners which mark the intersections of the lines which close thereon, and those from which the surveys start on the north. On these lines, and at the time of running the same, the township, section, and quarter-section corners are to be planted, and each of these is a corner common to *two*, (whether township or section corners,) on the north side of the line, and must be so marked.

The corners which are established on the standard parallel, at the time of running it, are to be known as "*standard corners*," and, in addition to all the *ordinary* marks, (as herein prescribed,) they will be marked with the letters S. C. Closing corners will be marked with the letters C. C. in addition to other marks.

The standard parallels are designed to be run *in advance* of the contiguous surveys on the south of them, but circumstances may exist which will *impede* or temporarily delay the *due* extension of the standard; and when, from uncontrollable causes, the *contiguous townships* must be surveyed in advance of the time of extending the standard, in any such event it will become the duty of the deputy who shall afterward survey any such standard to plant thereon the *double set* of corners, to wit, the standard corners, to be marked S. C., and the closing ones, which are to be marked C. C.; and to make such measurements as may be necessary to connect the closing corners and complete the unfinished meridional lines of such contiguous and prior surveys, on the principles herein set forth, under the different heads of "exterior or township lines," and of "Diagram B."

You will recollect that the corners (whether township or section corners) which are *common* to *two*, (two townships or two sections,) are not to be planted *diagonally* like those which are common to *four*, but with the flat sides facing the cardinal points, and on which the marks and notches are made as usual. This, it will be perceived, will serve yet more fully to distinguish the standard parallels from all other lines

THE MEANDERING OF NAVIGABLE STREAMS.

1. Standing with the face looking *down* stream, the bank on the *left* hand is termed the "left bank," and that on the *right* hand the "right bank." These terms are to be universally used to distinguish the two banks of a river or stream.

2. Both banks of *navigable* rivers are to be meandered by taking the courses and distances of their sinuosities, and the same are to be entered in the field-book.

At those points where either the township or section lines intersect the banks of a navigable stream, POSTS, or where necessary, MOUNDS of *earth* or *stone*, are to be established at the time of running these lines. These are called "meander corners;" and in meandering you are to commence at one of those corners on the township line, coursing the banks, and measuring the distance of each course from your commencing corner to the next "meander corner," upon the same or another boundary of the same township, carefully noting your intersection with all intermediate meander corners. By the same method you are to meander the opposite bank of the same river.

The crossing distance *between* the MEANDER CORNERS on same line is to be ascertained by triangulation, in order that the river may be protracted with entire accuracy. The particulars to be given in the field-notes.

3. You are also to meander, in manner aforesaid, all *lakes* and deep ponds of the area of twenty-five acres and upward; also navigable bayous; *shallow* ponds, readily to be drained, or likely to dry up, are not to be meandered.

You will notice all streams of water falling into the river, lake, or bayou you are surveying, stating the width of the same at their mouth; also all springs, noting the size thereof and depth, and whether the water be pure or mineral; also the head and mouth of all bayous; and all islands, rapids, and bars are to be noticed, with intersections to their upper and lower points to establish their exact situation. You will also note the elevation of the banks of rivers and streams, the heights of falls and cascades, and the length of rapids.

4. The precise relative position of islands, in a township made fractional by the river in which the same are situated, is to be determined trigonometrically; sighting to a flag or other fixed object on the island, from a special and carefully measured base line, connected with the surveyed lines, on or near the river bank, you are to form connection between the meander corners on the river to points corresponding thereto, in direct line, on the bank of the island, and there establish the proper meander corners, and calculate the distance across.

5. In meandering lakes, ponds, or bayous, you are to commence at a meander corner upon the township line, and proceed as above directed for the banks of a navigable stream. But where a lake, pond, or bayou lies entirely within the township boundaries, you will commence at a meander corner established in subdividing, and from thence take the courses and distances of the entire margin of the same, noting the intersection with all the meander corners previously established thereon.

6. To meander a pond lying entirely within the boundaries of a section, you will run and measure *two* lines thereunto from the nearest section or quarter-section corner on *opposite* sides of such pond, giving the courses of such lines. At *each* of the points where such lines shall intersect the margin of such pond, you will establish a *witness* point, by fixing a post in the ground, and taking bearings to any adjacent trees, or, if necessary, raising a mound.

The relative position of these points being thus definitely fixed in the section, the meandering will commence at one of them, and be continued to the other, noting the intersection, and thence to the beginning. The proceedings are to be fully entered in the field-book.

7. In taking the connection of an island with the main land, when there is no meander corner in line, opposite thereto, to sight from, you will measure a special base from the meander corner nearest to such island, and from such base you will triangulate to some fixed point on the shore of the island, ascertain the distance across, and there establish a *special* meander corner, wherefrom you will commence to meander the island.

8. The field notes of meanders will be set forth in the body of the field book according to the dates when the work is performed, as illustrated in the specimen notes annexed. They are to state and describe particularly the meander corner from which they commenced, each one with which they close, and are to exhibit the meanders of each fractional section separately; following, and composing a part of such notes, will be given a description of the land, timber, depth of inundation to which the bottom is subject, and the banks, current, and bottom of the stream or body of water you are meandering.

9. No blazes or marks of any description are to be made on the lines meandered between the established corners, but the utmost care must

be taken to pass no object of topography, *or change therein*, without giving a particular description thereof in its proper place in your meander notes.

OF FIELD BOOKS.

The FIELD NOTES afford the elements from which the plats and calculations in relation to the public surveys are made. They are the source wherefrom the description and evidence of locations and boundaries are officially delineated and set forth. They therefore must be a faithful, distinct, and minute record of everything officially done and observed by the surveyor and his assistants, pursuant to instructions, in relation to running, measuring, and making lines, establishing boundary corners, &c.; and present, as far as possible, a full and complete *topographical description* of the country surveyed, as to every matter of useful information, or likely to gratify public curiosity.

There will be sundry separate and distinct field books of surveys, as follows:

Field notes of the MERIDIAN and BASE lines, showing the establishment of the *township, section* or mile, and *quarter section* or half mile, boundary corners thereon; with the crossings of streams, ravines, hills, and mountains; character of soil, timber, minerals, &c.

Field notes of the "STANDARD PARALLELS, or correction lines," will show the establishment of the township, section, and quarter section corners, besides exhibiting the topography of the country on line, as required on the base and meridian lines.

Field notes of the EXTERIOR lines of TOWNSHIPS, showing the establishment of corners on lines, and the topography, as aforesaid.

Field notes of the SUBDIVISIONS of TOWNSHIPS into sections and quarter sections.

The field notes must in all cases be taken precisely in the order in which the work is done on the ground, and the *date* of each day's work must follow immediately after the notes thereof. The *variation of the needle* must always occupy a *separate line* preceding the notes of measurements on line.

The exhibition of every mile of surveying, whether on township or subdivisional lines, must be *complete in itself*, and be separated by a black line drawn across the paper.

The description of the surface, soil, minerals, timber, undergrowth, &c., on *each mile* of line, is to follow the notes of survey of such line, and not be mixed up with them.

No abbreviations of words are allowable, except of such words as are *constantly* occurring, such as "*sec.*" for "*section;*" "*in. diam,*" for "*inches diameter;*" "*chs.*" for "*chains;*" "*lks.*" for "*links;*" "*dist.*" for "*distant,*" &c. Proper names must never be abbreviated, however often their recurrence.

The nature of the subject-matter of the field book is to form its title page, showing the State or Territory where such survey lies, by whom surveyed, and the dates of commencement and completion of the work. The second page is to contain the names and duties of assistants. Whenever a new assistant is employed, or the duties of any one of them are changed, such facts, with the reason therefor, are to be stated in an appropriate entry immediately preceding the notes taken under such changed arrangements. With the notes of the *exterior* lines of townships, the deputy is to submit a plat of the lines run, on a scale of two inches to the mile, on which are to be noted all the objects of topography on line necessary to illustrate the notes, viz, the distance on line at the crossings of streams, so far as such can be noted on the paper, and the direction of each by an arrow-head pointing down stream; also the intersection of line by prairies, marshes, swamps, ravines, ponds, lakes, hills, mountains, and all other matters indicated by the notes, to the fullest extent practicable.

With the instructions for making subdivisional surveys of townships into sections, the deputy will be furnished by the surveyor general with a diagram of the *exterior* lines of the townships to be subdivided, (on the above-named scale,) upon which are carefully to be laid down the measurements of each of the section lines on such boundaries whereon he is to close, the magnetic variation of each mile, and the particular description of each corner. P. in M. signifies post in mound. And on such diagram the deputy who subdivides will make appropriate sketches of the various objects of topography as they occur on his lines, so as to exhibit not only the points on line at which the same occur, but also the direction and position of each between the lines, or within each section, so that every object of topography may be properly completed or connected in the showing.

These notes must be distinctly written out, in language precise and clear, and their figures, letters, words, and meaning are always to be unmistakable. No leaf is to be cut or mutilated, and none to be taken out, whereby suspicion might be created that the missing leaf contained matter which the deputy believed it to be his interest to conceal.

SUMMARY OF OBJECTS AND DATA REQUIRED TO BE NOTED.

1. The precise length of every line run, noting all necessary offsets therefrom, with the reason and mode thereof.

2. The kind and diameter of all "*bearing trees*," with the course and distance of the same from their respective corners; and the precise relative position of WITNESS CORNERS to the *true corners.*

3. The kind of materials (earth or stone) of which MOUNDS are constructed—the fact of their being conditioned according to instructions—with the course and distance of the "*pits*," from the center of the mound, where necessity exists for deviating from the *general* rule.

4. *Trees on line.* The name, diameter, and distance on line to all trees which it intersects.

5. Intersections by line of *land objects.* The distance at which the line first intersects and then leaves every *settler's claim and improvement;* prairie, river, creek, or other "bottom;" or swamp, marsh, grove, and wind fall, with the course of the same at both points of intersection; also the distances at which you begin to ascend, arrive at the top, begin to descend, and reach the foot of all remarkable hills and ridges, with their courses, and *estimated* height, in feet, above the level land of the surrounding country, or above the bottom lands, ravines, or waters near which they are situated.

6. Intersections by line of *water objects.* All rivers, creeks, and smaller streams of water which the line crosses; the distances on line at the points of intersection, and their *widths on line.* In cases of *navigable* streams, their width will be ascertained between the *meander corners,* as set forth under the proper head.

7. The land's *surface*—whether level, rolling, broken, or hilly.

8. The *soil*—whether first, second, or third rate.

9. *Timber*—the several kinds of timber and undergrowth, in the order in which they predominate.

10. *Bottom lands*—to be described as wet or dry, and if subject to inundation, state to what depth.

11. *Springs of water*—whether fresh, saline, or mineral, with the course of the stream flowing from them.

12. *Lakes* and *ponds*—describing their banks and giving their height, and also the depth of water, and whether it be pure or stagnant.

13. *Improvements.* Towns and villages; Indian towns and wigwams; houses or cabins; fields, or other improvements; sugar tree groves, sugar camps, mill seats, forges, and factories.

14. *Coal* banks or beds; *peat* or turf grounds; *minerals* and ores; with particular description of the same as to quality and extent, and all *diggings* therefor; also *salt* springs and licks. All reliable information you can obtain respecting these objects, whether they be on your immediate line or not, is to appear on the general description to be given at the end of the notes.

15. *Roads* and *trails*, with their directions, whence and whither.

16. Rapids, cataracts, cascades, or falls of water, with the height of their fall in feet.

17. Precipices, caves, sink-holes, ravines, stone quarries, ledges of rocks, with the kind of stone they afford.

18. *Natural curiosities*, interesting fossils, petrifactions, organic remains, &c.; also all ancient works of art, such as mounds, fortifications, embankments, ditches, or objects of like nature.

19. The *variation* of the needle must be noted at all points or places on the lines where there is found any material *change* of variation, and the position of such points must be perfectly identified in the notes.

20. Besides the ordinary notes taken on line, (and which must always be written down on the spot, leaving nothing to be supplied by memory,) the deputy will subjoin, at the conclusion of his book, such further description or information touching any matter or thing connected with the township (or other survey) which he may be able to afford, and may deem useful or necessary to be known—with a *general description* of the township in the *aggregate*, as respects the face of the country, its soil and geological features, timber, minerals, waters, &c.

SWAMP LANDS.

By the act of Congress approved September 28, 1850, swamp and overflowed lands "unfit for cultivation" are granted to the State in which they are situated. In order clearly to define the quantity and locality of such lands, the field notes of surveys, in addition to the other objects of topography required to be noted, are to indicate the points at which you enter all lands which are evidently subject to such grant, and to show the distinctive character of the land so noted; whether it is a swamp or marsh, or otherwise subject to inundation to an extent that, without artificial means, would render it "unfit for cultivation." The depth of inundation is to be stated, as determined from indications on the trees where timber exists; and its frequency is to be set forth as accurately as may be, either from your own knowledge of the general character of the stream which overflows, or from reliable information to be obtained from others. The words "unfit for cultivation" are to be employed in addition to the usual phraseology in regard to entering or leaving such swamps, marshy, or overflowed lands. It may be that sometimes the margin of bottom, swamp, or marsh, in which such uncultivable land exists, is not identical with the margin of the body of land "unfit for cultivation;" and in such cases a separate entry must be made for each opposite the marginal distance at which they respectively occur.

But in cases where lands are overflowed by *artificial* means, (say by dams for milling, logging, or for other purposes,) you are not officially to regard such overflow, but will continue your lines across the same without setting meander posts, stating particularly in the notes the depth of the water, and how the overflow was caused.

SPECIAL INSTRUCTION RESPECTING THE NOTING OF SETTLERS' CLAIMS IN OREGON, WASHINGTON, AND NEW MEXICO.

The law requires that such claims should be laid down temporarily on the township plats; in order to do which, it is indispensably necessary to obtain, to some extent, connections of these claims with the lines of survey. Under the head of "intersection by line of land objects," the deputy is required to note the *points* in line *whereat* it may be intersected by such claims; but, in addition thereto, there must be obtained at least *one angle* of each claim, with its course and distance either from the point of intersection, or from an established corner boundary, so that its connection with the regular survey will be legally determined. If the settler's *dwelling* or barn is visible from line, the bearings thereof should be carefully taken from *two* points noted on line, and set forth in the field notes.

AFFIDAVITS TO FIELD NOTES.

At the close of the notes and the *general description* is to follow an affidavit, a form for which is given; and to enable the deputy surveyor fully to understand and appreciate the responsibility under which he is acting, his attention is invited to the provisions of the second section of the act of Congress, approved August 8th, 1846, entitled "An act to equalize the compensation of the surveyors general of the public lands of the United States, and for other purposes," and which is as follows:

"SEC. 2. That the surveyors general of the public lands of the United States, in addition to the oath now authorized by law to be administered to deputies on their appointment to office, shall require each of their deputies, on the return of his surveys, to take and subscribe an oath or affirmation that those surveys have been faithfully and correctly executed according to law and the instructions of the surveyor general; and on satisfactory evidence being presented to any court of competent jurisdiction that such surveys, or any part thereof, had not been thus executed, the deputy making such false oath or affirmation shall be deemed guilty of perjury, and shall suffer all the pains and penalties attached to that offense; and the district attorney of the United States for the time being, in whose district any such false, erroneous, or fraudulent surveys shall have been executed, shall, upon the application of the proper surveyor general, immediately institute suit upon the bond of such deputy; and the institution of such suit shall act as a lien upon any property owned or held by such deputy, or his sureties, at the time such suit was instituted."

Following the "general description" of the township is to be "A list of the names of the individuals employed to assist in running, measuring, and marking the lines and corners described in the foregoing field notes of township No. ―――― of the BASE LINE of range No. ―――― of the ―――― MERIDIAN, showing the respective capacities in which they acted."

FORM OF OFFICIAL OATHS TO BE TAKEN PRIOR TO ENTERING UPON DUTY.

For a deputy surveyor.

I, A B, having been appointed a deputy surveyor of the lands of the United States in ———, do solemnly swear (or affirm) that I will well and faithfully, and to the best of my skill and ability, execute the duties confided to me pursuant to a contract with C D, surveyor general of public lands in ———, bearing date the ——— day of ———, 18 —, according to the laws of the United States and the instructions received from the said surveyor general.

(To be sworn and subscribed before a justice of the peace, or other officer authorized to administer oaths.)

For chainman.

I, E F, do solemnly swear (or affirm) that I will faithfully execute the duties of chain carrier; that I will level the chain upon uneven ground, and plumb the tally pins, whether by sticking or dropping the same; that I will report the true distance to all notable objects, and the true length of all lines that I assist in measuring, to the best of my skill and ability.

(To be sworn and subscribed as above.)

For flagman or axman.

I, G H, do solemnly swear (or affirm) that I will well and truly perform the duties of ———, according to instructions given me, and to the best of my skill and ability.

(To be sworn and subscribed as above.)

EXTERIORS OR TOWNSHIP LINES.

The principal meridian, the base line, and the standard parallels having been first run, measured, and marked, and the corner boundaries thereon established, according to instructions, the process of running, measuring, and marking the exterior lines of townships will be as follows:

Townships situated NORTH *of the base line and* WEST *of the principal meridian.*

Commence at No. 1, (see figures on Diagram A,) being the southwest corner of T. 1 N.—R. 1 W., as established on the base line; thence north, on a true meridian line, four hundred and eighty chains, establishing the section and quarter-section corners thereon, as per instructions, to No. 2, whereat establish the corner of Tps. 1 and 2 N.—Rs. 1 and 2 W.; thence east, on a random or trial line, setting *temporary* section and quarter-section stakes, to No. 3, where measure and note the distance at which the line intersects the eastern boundary, north or south of the *true* or established corner. Run and measure westward, on the true line, (taking care to note all the land and water crossings, &c., as per instructions,) to No. 4, which is identical with No. 2, establishing the section and quarter-section PERMANENT CORNERS on said line.

Should it happen, however, that such random line falls short, or overruns in length, or intersects the eastern boundary of the township at more than three chains and fifty links distance from the *true* corner thereon, as compared with the corresponding boundary on the south, (either of which would indicate an important error in the surveying,) the lines must be *retraced*, even if found necessary to remeasure the meridional boundaries of the township, (especially the western boundary,) so as to discover and correct the error; in doing which, the *true corners* must be established and marked, and the *false ones* destroyed and obliterated to prevent confusion in future; and *all the facts* must be distinctly set forth in the notes. Thence proceed in a similar manner from No. 4 to No. 5, No. 5 to No. 6, No. 6 to No. 7, and so on to No. 10, the southwest corner of T. 4 N.—R. 1 W. Thence north, still on a true meridian line, establishing the mile and half-mile corners, until reaching the STANDARD PARALLEL or correction line; throwing the *excess* over, or *deficiency* under, *four hundred and eighty chains*, on the *last* half-mile, according to law, and at the intersection establishing the "CLOSING CORNER," the distance of which *from* the standard corner must be measured and noted as required by the instructions. But should it ever so happen that some impassable barrier will have prevented or delayed the extension of the standard parallel along and above the field of present survey, then the deputy will plant, in place, the corner for the township, subject to correction thereafter, should such parallel be extended.

NORTH *of the base line, and* EAST *of the principal meridian.*

Commence at No. 1, being the *southeast* corner of T. 1 N.—R. 1 E., and proceed as with townships situated "north and west," except that the *random* or trial lines will be run and measured *west*, and the *true* lines east, throwing the excess over or deficiency under four hundred and eighty chains on the *west end* of the line, as required by law; wherefore the surveyor will commence his measurement with the length of the deficient or excessive half-section boundary on the west of the township, and thus the remaining measurements will all be *even* miles and half-miles.

METHOD OF SUBDIVIDING.

1. The first mile, both of the south and east boundaries of each township you are required to subdivide, is to be carefully traced and measured before you enter upon the subdivision thereof. This will enable you to observe any change that may have taken place in the magnetic variation, as it existed at the time of running the township lines, and will also enable you to compare your chaining with that upon the township lines.

2. Any discrepancy arising either from a change in the magnetic variation or a difference in measurement, is to be carefully noted in the field-notes.

3. After adjusting your compass to a variation which you have thus found will retrace the eastern boundary of the township, you will commence at the corner to sections 35 and 36, on the south boundary, and run a line due north, forty chains, to the quarter-section corner, which you are to establish between sections 35 and 36; continuing due north forty chains farther, you will establish the corner to sections 25, 26, 35, and 36.

4. From the section corner last named run a *random* line, without blazing, *due east*, for the corner of sections 25 and 36, in east boundary, and at forty chains from the starting point set a post for *temporary* quarter-section corner. If you intersect exactly at the corner, you will blaze your random line back, and establish it as the *true* line; but if your random line intersects the said east boundary, either north or south of said corner, you will measure the distance of such intersection, from which you will calculate a course that will run a *true* line back to the corner from which your random started. You will establish the *permanent* quarter-section corner at a point equidistant from the two terminations of the *true* line.

5. From the corner of sections 25, 26, 35, 36, run due north between sections 25 and 26, setting the quarter-section post as before, at forty chains, and at eighty chains establishing the corner of sections 23, 24, 25, 26. Then run a random *due east* for the corner of sections 24 and 25 in east boundary; setting temporary quarter-section post at forty chains; correcting back, and establishing *permanent* quarter-section corner at the equidistant point on the *true* line, in the manner directed on the line between sections 25 and 36.

6. In this manner you will proceed with the survey of each successive section in the first tier, until you arrive at the north boundary of the township, which you will reach in running up a random line between sections 1 and 2. If this random line should not intersect at the corner established for sections 1, 2, 35, and 36, upon the township line, you will note the distance that you fall east or west of the same, from which distance you will calculate a course that will run a true line south to the corner from which your random started. Where the closing corner is on the base or standard line, a deviation from the general rule is explained under the head of "Diagram B."

7. The first tier of sections being thus laid out and surveyed, you will return to the south boundary of the township, and from the corner of sections 34 and 35 commence and survey the second tier of sections in the same manner that you pursued in the survey of the first, closing at the section corners on the first tier.

8. In like manner proceed with the survey of each successive tier of sections, until you arrive at the fifth tier; and from each section corner which you establish upon this tier, you are to run random lines to the corresponding corners established upon the range line forming the western boundary of the township; setting, as you proceed, each *temporary* quarter-section post at forty chains from the interior section corner, so as to throw the excess or deficiency of measurement on the extreme tier of quarter sections contiguous to the township boundary; and on returning establish the *true* line, and establish thereon the *permanent* quarter-section corner.

QUARTER-SECTION CORNERS, both upon north and south and upon east and west lines, are to be established at a point *equidistant* from the corresponding section corners, *except* upon the lines closing on the north and west boundaries of the township, and in those situations the quarter-section corners will always be established at precisely *forty chains* to the north or west (as the case may be) of the respective section corners from which those lines respectively *start*, by which procedure the excess or deficiency in the measurements will be thrown, according to law, on the extreme tier of quarter sections.

Every north and south section line, except those terminating in the north boundary of the township, is to be eighty chains in length. The east and west section lines, except those terminating on the west boundary of the township, are to be within one hundred links of eighty chains in length; and the north and south boundaries of any one section, except in the extreme western tier, are to be within one hundred links of equal length. The meanders within each fractional section, or between any two meander posts, or of a pond or island in the interior of a section, must close within one chain and fifty links.

DIAGRAM A illustrates the mode of laying off township exteriors *north* of the BASE line and EAST and WEST of the principal MERIDIAN, whether between the base and first standard, or between any two standards; and the same general principles will equally apply to townships *south* of the base line and east and west of the meridian, and between any two standards *south*, where the distances between the base and first standard, and between the standards themselves, are five townships or thirty miles.

DIAGRAM B indicates the mode of laying off a TOWNSHIP into sections and quarter sections, and the accompanying set of field notes (marked B) critically illustrate the mode and order of conducting the survey under every variety of circumstance shown by the topography on the diagram. In townships lying *south* of and *contiguous* to the base or to any standard parallel, the lines between the northern tier of sections will be run *north*, and be made to close as *true* lines; quarter section corners will be set at forty chains, and section corners established at the intersection of such section lines with the base or standard, (as the case may be,) and the distance is to be measured and entered in the field book to the nearest corner on such standard or base.

DIAGRAM C illustrates the mode of making mound, a stake, or stone corner boundaries for townships, sections, and quarter sections.

The mode and order of surveying the *exterior* boundaries of a township are illustrated by the specimen field notes marked A; and the mode and order of *subdividing* a township into sections and quarter sections are illustrated by the specimen field notes marked B. The attention of the deputy is particularly directed to these specimens, as indicating not only the method in which his work is to be conducted, but also the order, manner, language, &c., in which his field notes are required to be returned to the surveyor general's office; and such specimens are to be deemed part of these instructions, and any *departure* from their details, without special authority, in cases where the circumstances are analogous in practice, *will be regarded as a violation of his contract and oath.*

The subdivisions of fractional sections into forty acre lots, (as near as may be,) are to be so laid down on the official township plat in *red* lines, as to admit of giving to each a specific designation, if possible, according to its relative position in the fractional section, as per examples afforded by Diagram B, as well as by a number, in all cases where the lot cannot properly be designated as a quarter-quarter. Those fractional subdivision lots which are not susceptible of being described according to relative local position, are to be numbered in regular series; No. 1 being (wherever practicable, and as a general rule) either the northeastern or the most easterly fractional lot, and proceeding from east to west and from west to east, alternately, to the end of the series; but such general rule is departed from under circumntances given as examples in fractional sections 4, 7, 19 and 30, where No. 1 is the interior lot of the northern and western tiers of the quarter sections to which there is a corresponding No. 2 given to the exterior lot, and the series of numbers is in continuation of the latter. The lots in the extreme northern and western tiers of quarter sections, containing either more or less than the regular quantity, are always to be numbered as per example. Interior lots in such extreme tiers are to be *twenty* chains wide, and the excess or deficiency of measurement is always to be thrown on the exterior lots; elsewhere, the assumed subdivisional corner will always be a point equidistant from the established corners.

The official township plat to be returned to the General Land Office is to show on its face, on the right hand margin, the meanders of navigable streams, islands, and lakes. Such details are wanted in the adjustment of the surveying accounts, but may be omitted in the copy of the township plat to be furnished to the district land office by the surveyor general. A suitable margin for *binding* is to be preserved on the left hand side of each plat. Each plat is to be certified, with table annexed, according to the forms subjoined to "Diagram B," and is to show the areas of public land, of private surveys, and of water, with the aggregate area as shown on the diagram.

Each township plat is to be prepared in *triplicate:* one for the General Land Office, one for the district office, and the third to be retained as the record in the office of the surveyor general.

The original field books, each bearing the *written approval* of the surveyor general, are to be substantially bound into volumes of suitable size, and retained in the surveyor general's office, and certified *transcripts* of such field books (to be of *foolscap* size) are to be prepared and forwarded, from time to time, to the General Land Office.

With the copy of each township plat furnished to a district land office, the surveyor general is required by law to furnish *descriptive notes* as to the character and quality of the soil and timber found on and in the vicinity of each surveyed line, and giving a description of each corner boundary.

Printed blank forms for such notes will be furnished by the General Land Office. The forms provide eighteen spaces for *meander corners*, which, in most cases, will be sufficient; but when the number shall exceed eighteen, the residue will have to be inserted on the face of the township plat, to be furnished to the register of the district land office. There is shown a series of meander corners on Diagram B, viz., from No. 1 to No. 22, on the river and islands; 23 to 28 being on Island Lake; 29 and 30 on Clear Lake; and 31 and 32 on lake in section 26.

There is also a distinct series of numbers, 1 to 7, to designate corners to D. Reed's private survey, and to fractional sections, made such thereby; and the same series is continued from 8 to 14 inclusive, to designate corners to S. William's private survey, and to fractional sections made such thereby. These are numberings on the plat merely for the purpose of ready reference to the descriptions of such corners to be furnished to the registers.

The *letters* on "Diagram B," at the "corners" on the township boundaries, are referred to in the descriptive notes to be furnished to the district land office, but are not required to be inserted on the official plat to be returned to the General Land Office.

The following chapter, on the subject of the variation of the magnetic needle, is extracted from the revised edition of the work on surveying by Charles Davies, L. LD., a graduate of the Military Academy at

West Point. The work itself will be a valuable acquisition to the deputy surveyor; and his attention is particularly invited to the following chapter, which sets forth the modes by which the variation may be ascertained.

VARIATION OF THE NEEDLE.

1. The angle which the magnetic meridian makes with the true meridian, at any place on the surface of the earth, is called the *variation of the needle* at that place, and is east or west, according as the north end of the needle lies on the east or west side of the true meridian.

2. The variation is different at different places, and even at the same place it does not remain constant for any length of time. The variation is ascertained by comparing the magnetic with the true meridian.

3. If we suppose a line to be traced through those points on the surface of the earth, where the needle points directly north, such a line is called the *line of no variation*. At all places lying on the east of this line, the variation of the needle is west; at all places lying on the west of it, the variation is east.

4. The public is much indebted to Professor Loomis for the valuable results of many observations and much scientific research on the dip and variation of the needle, contained in the 39th and 42d volumes of Silliman's Journal.

The variation at each place was ascertained for the year 1840; and by a comparison of previous observations and the application of known formulas, the annual motion, or change in variation, at each place, was also ascertained, and both are contained in the tables which follow.

5. If the annual motion was correctly found, and continues uniform, the variation at any subsequent period can be ascertained by simply multiplying the annual motion by the number of years, and adding the product, in the algebraic sense, to the variation in 1840. It will be observed that all variations west are designated by the plus sign; and all variations east, by the minus sign. The annual motions being all west, have all the plus sign.

6. Our first object will be to mark the line, as it was in 1840, of *no variation*. For this purpose we shall make a table of places lying near this line:

Places near the line of no variation.

Place.	Latitude.	Longitude.	Variation.	Annual motion.
A Point	40° 53'	80° 13'	0° 00'	+4'.4
Cleveland, Ohio	41 31	81 45	—0 19	4. 4
Detroit, Michigan	42 24	82 58	—1 56	4
Mackinaw	45 51	84 41	—2 08	3. 9
Marietta, Ohio	39 30	81 28	—1 24	4. 3
Charlottesville, Virginia	39 02	78 30	+0 19	3. 7
Charleston, South Carolina	32 42	80 04	—2 44	1. 3

At the point whose latitude is 40° 53', longitude 80° 13', the variation of the needle was nothing in the year 1840, and the direction of the line of no variation, traced north, was N. 24° 35' west. The line of no variation, prolonged, passed a little to the east at Cleveland, in Ohio— the variation then being 19' east. Detroit lay still farther to the west of this line, the variation there being 1° 56' east; and Mackinaw still farther to the west, as the variation at that place was 2° 8' east.

The course of the line of no variation, prolonged sontherly, was S. 24° 35′ E. Marietta, Ohio, was west of this line—the variation there being 1° 24′ east. Charlottesville, in Virginia, was a little to the east of it—the variation there being 19′ west; whilst Charleston, in South Carolina, was on the west—the variation there being 2° 44′ east. From these results, it will be easy to see about where the line of no variation is traced in our own country.

7. We shall give two additional tables:

Places where the variation was west.

Places.	Latitude.	Longitude.	Variation.	Annual motion.
Angle of Maine	48° 00′	67° 37′	+19° 30′	+8′.8
Waterville, Maine	44 27	69 32	12 36	5.7
Montreal	45 31	73 35	10 18	5.7
Keesville, New York	44 28	73 32	8 51	5.3
Burlington, Vermont	44 27	73 10	9 27	5.3
Hanover, New Hampshire	43 42	72 14	9 20	5.2
Cambridge, Massachusetts	42 22	71 08	9 12	5
Hartford, Connecticut	41 46	72 41	6 58	5
Newport, Rhode Island	41 28	71 21	7 45	5
Geneva, New York	42 52	77 03	4 18	4.1
West Point	41 25	74 00	6 52	4
New York City	40 43	71 01	5 34	3.6
Philadelphia	39· 57	75 11	4 08	3.2
Buffalo, New York	42 52	79 06	1 37	4.1

Places where the variation was east.

Places.	Latitude.	Longitude.	Variation.	Annual motion.
Mouth of Columbia River	46° 12′	123° 30′	−21° 40′	Unknown.
Jacksonville, Illinois	39 43	90 20	8 28	+2′.5
St. Louis, Missouri	38 37	90 17	8 37	2.3
Nashville, Tennessee	36 10	86 52	6 42	2
Louisiana, at	29 40	94 00	8 41	1.4
Mobile, Alabama	30 42	88 16	7 05	1.4
Tuscaloosa, Alabama	33 12	87 43	7 26	1.6
Columbus, Georgia	32 28	85 11	5 28	2
Milledgeville, Georgia	33 07	83 24	5 07	2.4
Savannah, Georgia	32 05	81 12	4 13	2.7
Tallahassee, Florida	30 26	84 27	5 03	1.8
Pensacola, Florida	30 24	87 23	5 53	1.4
Logansport, Indiana	40 45	86 22	5 24	2.7
Cincinnati, Ohio	39 06	84 27	4 46	3.1

METHODS OF ASCERTAINING THE VARIATION.

8. The best practical method of determining the true meridian of a place is by observing the north star. If this star were precisely at the point in which the axis of the earth, prolonged, pierces the heavens, then the intersection of the vertical plane passing through it and the place, with the surface of the earth, would be the true meridian. But the star being at a distance from the pole equal to 1° 30′ nearly, it performs a revolution about the pole in a circle, the polar distance of which is 1° 30′: the time of revolution is 23 h. and 56 min.

To the eye of an observer this star is continually in motion, and is due north but twice in 23 h. 56 min.; and is then said to be on the meridian. Now, when it departs from the meridian it apparently moves east or west for 5h. and 59 m., and then returns to the meridian again. When at its greatest distance from the meridian, east or west, it is said to be at its greatest *eastern* or *western* elongation.

The following tables show the times of its greatest eastern and western elongations.

Eastern elongations.

Days.	April.	May.	June.	July.	August.	Sept.
	h. m.	h. m.	h. m.	h. m.	h. m.	h. m.
1	18 18	16 26	14 24	12 20	10 16	8 20
7	17 56	16 03	14 00	11 55	9 53	7 58
13	17 34	15 40	13 35	11 31	9 30	7 36
19	17 12	15 17	13 10	11 07	9 08	7 15
25	16 49	14 53	12 45	10 43	8 45	6 53

Western elongations.

Days.	Oct.	Nov.	Dec.	Jan.	Feb.	March.
	h. m.	h. m.	h. m.	h. m.	h. m.	h. m.
1	18 18	16 22	14 19	12 02	9 50	8 01
7	17 56	15 59	13 53	11 36	9 26	7 38
13	17 34	15 35	13 27	11 10	9 02	7 16
19	17 12	15 10	13 00	10 44	8 39	6 54
25	16 49	14 45	12 34	10 18	8 16	6 33

The eastern elongations are put down from the first of April to the first of October; and the western from the first of October to the first of April; the time is computed from 12 at noon. The western elongations in the first case, and the eastern in the second, occurring in the daytime, cannot be used. Some of those put down are also invisible, occurring in the evening, before it is dark, or after daylight in the morning. In such case, if it be necessary to determine the meridian at that particular season of the year, let 5 h. and 59 m. be added to, or subtracted from, the time of greatest eastern or western elongation, and the observation be made at night, when the star is on the meridian.

9. The following table exhibits the angle which the meridian plane makes with the vertical plane passing through the pole-star, when at its greatest eastern or western elongation: such angle is called the *azimuth*. The mean angle only is put down, being calculated for the first of July of each year:

Azimuth table.

Year.	Lat. 32° Azimuth.	Lat. 34° Azimuth.	Lat. 36° Azimuth.	Lat. 38° Azimuth.	Lat. 40° Azimuth.	Lat. 42° Azimuth.	Lat. 44° Azimuth.
1851......	1° 45½′	1° 48′	1° 50½′	1° 53½′	1° 56¾′	2° 00¼′	2° 04¼′
1852......	1° 45′	1° 47½′	1° 50′	1° 53′	1° 56¼′	1° 59¾′	2° 03¾′
1853......	1° 44½′	1° 47′	1° 49¾′	1° 52½′	1° 55¾′	1° 59¼′	2° 03¼′
1854......	1° 44¼′	1° 46½′	1° 49¼′	1° 52′	1° 55¼′	1° 59′	2° 02¾′
1855......	1° 43¾′	1° 46¼′	1° 48¾′	1° 51¾′	1° 54¾′	1° 58½′	2° 02¼′
1856......	1° 43¼′	1° 45¾′	1° 48¼′	1° 51¼′	1° 54½′	1° 58′	2° 01¾′
1857......	1° 43′	1° 45¼′	1° 48′	1° 50¾′	1° 54′	1° 57½′	2° 01¼′
1858......	1° 42½′	1° 44¾′	1° 47½′	1° 50¼′	1° 53½′	1° 57′	2° 00¾′
1859......	1° 42′	1° 44½′	1° 47′	1° 49¾′	1° 53′	1° 56½′	2° 00¼′
1860......	1° 41¾′	1° 44′	1° 46½′	1° 49½′	1° 52½′	1° 56′	2° 00′
1861......	1° 41¼′	1° 43¾′	1° 46¼′	1° 49′	1° 52¼′	1° 55¾′	1° 59¼′

The use of the above tables, in finding the true meridian, will soon appear.

TO FIND THE TRUE MERIDIAN WITH THE THEODOLITE.

10. Take a board, of about one foot square, paste white paper upon it, and perforate it through the center; the diameter of the hole being somewhat larger than the diameter of the telescope of the theodolite. Let this board be so fixed to a vertical staff as to slide up and down freely; and let a small piece of board, about three inches square, be nailed to the lower edge of it, for the purpose of holding a candle.

About twenty-five minutes before the time of the greatest eastern or western elongation of the pole-star, as shown by the tables of elongations, let the theodolite be placed at a convenient point and leveled. Let the board be placed about one foot in front of the theodolite, a lamp or candle placed on the shelf at its lower edge; and let the board be slipped up or down, until the pole-star can be seen through the hole. The light reflected from the paper will show the cross hairs in the telescope of the theodolite.

Then, let the vertical spider's line be brought exactly upon the pole-star, and, if it is an eastern elongation that is to be observed, and the star has not yet reached the most easterly point, it will move from the line toward the east, and the reverse when the elongation is west.

At the time the star attains its greatest elongation, it will appear to coincide with the vertical spider's line for some time, and then leave it, in the direction contrary to its former motion.

As the star moves toward the point of greatest elongation, the telescope must be continually directed to it, by means of the tangent-screw of the vernier plate; and when the star has attained its greatest elongation, great care should be taken that the instrument be not afterward moved.

Now, if it be not convenient to leave the instrument in its place until daylight, let a staff, with a candle or small lamp upon its upper extremity, be arranged at thirty or forty yards from the theodolite, and in the same vertical plane with the axis of the telescope. This is easily effected, by revolving the vertical limb about its horizontal axis without moving the vernier plate, and aligning the staff to coincide with the vertical hair. Then mark the point directly under the theodolite; the line passing through this point and the staff, makes an angle with the true meridian equal to the azimuth of the pole-star.

From the table of azimuths, take the azimuth corresponding to the year and nearest latitude. If the observed elongation was east, the true meridian lies on the west of the line which has been found, and makes with it an angle equal to the azimuth. If the elongation was west, the true meridian lies on the east of the line; and, in either case, laying off the azimuth angle with the theodolite, gives the true meridian.

TO FIND THE TRUE MERIDIAN WITH THE COMPASS.

11. 1. Drive two posts firmly into the ground, in a line nearly east and west; the uppermost ends, after the posts are driven, being about three feet above the surface, and the posts about four feet apart; then lay a plank, or piece of timber three or four inches in width, and smooth on the upper side, upon the posts, and let it be pinned or nailed, to hold it firmly.

2. Prepare a piece of board four or five inches square, and smooth on the under side. Let one of the compass-sights be placed at right angles to the upper surface of the board, and let a nail be driven through the board, so that it can be tacked to the timber resting on the posts.

3. At about twelve feet from the stakes, and in the direction of the pole-star, let a plumb be suspended from the top of an inclined stake or pole. The top of the pole should be of such a height that the pole star will appear about six inches below it; and the plumb should be swung in a vessel of water to prevent it from vibrating.

This being done, about twenty minutes before the time of elongation, place the board to which the compass-sight is fastened on the horizontal plank, and slide it east or west, until the aperture of the compass-sight, the plumb-line, and the star are brought into the same range. Then if the star depart from the plumb-line, move the compass-sight east or west along the timber, as the case may be, until the star shall attain its greatest elongation, when it will continue behind the plumb-line for several minutes, and will then recede from it in the direction contrary to its motion before it became stationary. Let the compass-sight be now fastened to the horizontal plank. During this observation it will be necessary to have the plumb-line lighted: this may be done by an assistant holding a candle near it.

Let now a staff, with a candle or lamp upon it, be placed at a distance of thirty or forty yards from the plumb-line, and in the same direction with it and the compass-sight. The line so determined makes, with the true meridian, an angle equal to the azimuth of the pole star; and from this line the variation of the needle is readily determined, even without tracing the true meridian on the ground.

Place the compass upon this line, turn the sights in the direction of it, and note the angle shown by the needle. Now, if the elongation at the time of observation was west, and the north end of the needle is on the west side of the line, the azimuth, plus the angle shown by the needle, is the true variation. But should the north end of the needle be found on the east side of the line, the elongation being west, the difference between the azimuth and the angle would show the variation, and the reverse when the elongation is east.

1. Elongation west, azimuth .... 2° 04'
   North end of the needle on the west, angle .... 4° 06'

   Variation .. .. 6° 10' west.

2. Elongation west, azimuth .... 1° 59'
   North end of the needle on the east, angle .... 4° 50'

   Variation .... 2° 51' east.

3. Elongation east, azimuth .... 2° 05'
   North end of the needle on the west, angle .... 8° 30'

   Variation .... 6° 25' west.

4. Elongation east, azimuth .... 1° 57'
   North end of the needle on the east, angle .... 8° 40'

   Variation .... 10° 37' east.

REMARK I.—The variation at West Point, in September, 1835, was 6° 32' west.

REMARK II.—The variation of the needle should always be noted on every survey made with the compass, and then if the land be surveyed at a future time, the old lines can always be re-run.

12. It has been found by observation, that heat and cold sensibly affect the magnetic needle, and that the same needle will at the same place indicate different lines at different hours of the day.

If the magnetic meridian be observed early in the morning, and again at different hours of the day, it will be found that the needle will continue to recede from the meridian as the day advances, until about the time of the highest temperature, when it will begin to return, and at evening will make the same line as in the morning. This change is called the *diurnal variation,* and varies, during the summer season, from one-fourth to one-fifth of a degree.

13. A very near approximation to a true meridian, and consequently to the variation, may be had, by remembering that the pole star very nearly reaches the true meridian, when it is in the same vertical plane with the star Alioth in the tail of the Great Bear, which lies nearest the four stars forming the quadrilateral.

The vertical position can be ascertained by means of a plumb-line. To see the spider's lines in the field of the telescope at the same time with the star, a faint light should be placed near the object-glass. When the plumb-line, the star Alioth, and the north star, fall on the vertical spider's line, the horizontal limb is firmly clamped, and the telescope brought down to the horizon; a light, seen through a small aperture in a board, and held at some distance by an assistant, is then moved according to signals, until it is covered by the intersection of the spider's lines. A picket driven into the ground, under the light, serves to mark the meridian line for reference by day, when the angle formed by it and the magnetic meridian may be measured.

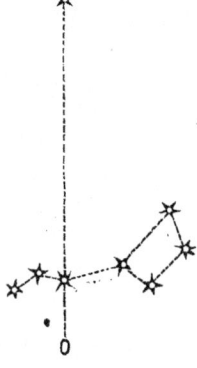

A.

FIELD-NOTES OF THE SURVEY OF THE EXTERIOR BOUNDARIES OF TOWNSHIP 25 NORTH, OF RANGE 2 WEST, OF THE WILLAMETTE MERIDIAN, IN THE TERRITORY OF OREGON, BY ROBERT ACRES, DEPUTY SURVEYOR, UNDER HIS CONTRACT No. 1, BEARING DATE THE 2D DAY OF JANUARY, 1854.

South boundary, T. 25 N., R. 2 W., Willamette meridian.

Chains.	
	Begin at the post, the established corner to townships 24 and 25 north, in ranges 2 and 3 west. The witness trees all standing, and agree with the description furnished me by the office, viz:
	A black oak, 20 in. dia., N. 37 E. 27 links;
	A bur oak, 24 in. dia., N. 43 W. 35 links;
	A maple, 18 in. dia., S. 27 W. 39 links;
	A white oak, 15 in. dia., S. 47 E. 41 links.
	East, on a random line on the south boundaries of sections 31, 32, 33, 34, 35, and 36,
	Variation by Burt's improved solar compass, 18° 41' E.,
	I set temporary half-mile and mile posts at every 40 and 80 chains; and at 5 miles 74 chains 53 links, to a point 2 chains and 20 links north of the corner to townships 24 and 25 north, ranges 1 and 2 W.,
	(Therefore the correction will be 5 chains 47 links *west* and 37 links *south* per mile,)
	I find the corner post standing, and the witness trees to agree with the description furnished me by the surveyor general's office, viz:
	A bur oak, 17 in. dia., bears N. 44 E. 31 links;
	A white oak, 16 in. dia., N. 26 W. 21 links;
	A lynn, 20 in. dia., S. 42 W. 15 links;
	A black oak, 24 in. dia., S. 27 E. 14 links.
	From the corner to townships 24 and 25 N., ranges 1 and 2 west, I run (at a variation of 18° 25' east)
	West, on a *true* line along the south boundary of section 36,
40.00	Set a post for quarter-section corner, from which
	A beech, 24 in. dia., bears N. 11 E., 38 links dist.;
	A beech, 9 in. dia., bears S. 9 E., 17 links dist.
62.59	A brook, 6 links wide, runs north.
80.00	Set a post for corner to sections 35 and 36, 1 and 2, from which
	A beech, 9 in. dia., bears N. 22 E., 16 links dist.;
	A beech, 8 in. dia., bears N. 19 W., 14 links dist.;
	A white oak, 10 in. dia., bears S. 52 W., 7 links dist.;
	A black oak, 14 in. dia., bears S. 46 E., 8 links dist.
	Land level, good soil, fit for cultivation.
	Timber, beech; various kinds of oak, ash, and hickory.
	West, on a *true* line along the south boundary of section 35, Variation 18° 25' east,
40.00	Set a post for quarter-section corner, from which
	A beech, 8 in. dia., bears N. 20 E., 8 links dist.
	No other tree convenient; made trench around post.
65.00	Begin to ascend a moderate hill; bears N. and S.
80.00	Set a post with trench for corner of sections 34 and 35, 2 and 3, from which
	A beech, 10 in. dia., bears N. 56 W., 9 links dist.;
	A beech, 10 in. dia., bears S. 51 E., 13 links dist.
	No other trees convenient to mark.
	Land level, or gently rolling, and good for farming.
	Timber, beech, oak, ash, and hickory; some walnut and poplar.
	West, on a *true* line along the south boundary of section 34, Variation 18° 25' east,
40.00	Set a quarter-section post with trench, from which

INDEX.

Referring the lines to the pages of the field-notes.

Town. 25 N. Range 2 W. Willamette Meridian.

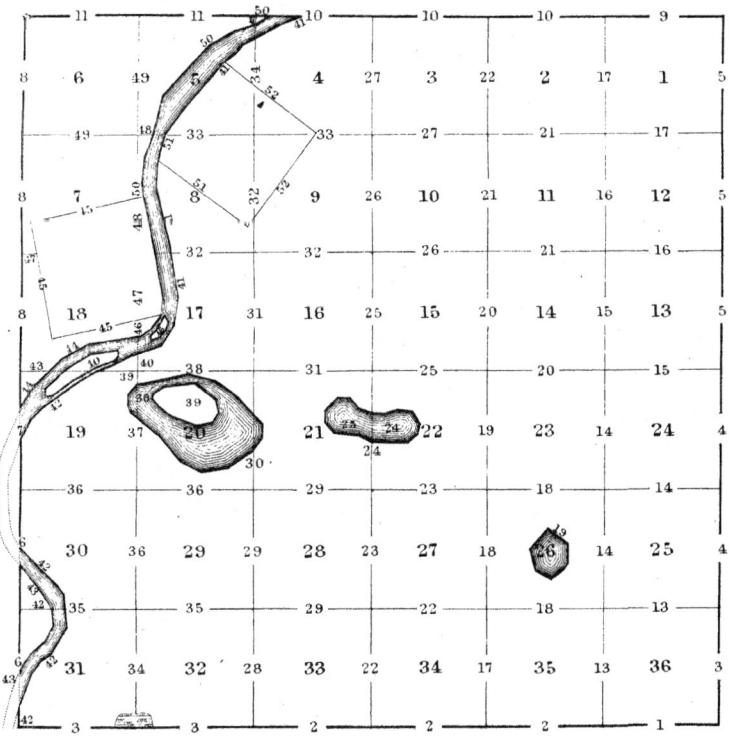

South boundary, T. 25 N., R. 2 W., Willamette meridian—Continued.

Chains.	
	A black oak, 10 in. dia., bears N. 2 E., 635 links dist.
	No other tree convenient to mark.
80.00	To point for corner of sections 33, 34, 3 and 4,
	Drove charred stakes, raised mounds with trenches, as per instructions, from which
	A bur oak, 16 in. dia., bears N. 31 E. 344 links; and
	A hickory, 12 in. dia., bears S. 43 W. 231 links.
	No other trees convenient to mark.
	Land level, rich, and good for farming.
	Timber, some scattering oak and walnut.
	West, on a *true* line along the south boundary of section 33,
	Variation 18° 25′ east,
37.51	A black oak, 24 in. dia.
40.00	Set a post for quarter-section corner, from which
	A black oak, 18 in. dia., bears N. 25 E., 32 links dist.;
	A white oak, 15 in. dia., bears N. 43 W., 22 links dist.
62.00	To foot of steep hill, bears N. E. and S. W.
80.00	Set a post for corner to sections 32, 33, 4 and 5, from which
	A white oak, 15 in. dia., bears N. 23 E., 27 links dist.;
	A black oak, 20 in. dia., bears N. 82 W., 75 links dist.;
	A bur oak, 20 in. dia., bears S. 37 W., 92 links dist.;
	A white oak, 24 in. dia., bears S. 26 E., 42 links dist.
	Land gently rolling; good rich land for farming.
	Timber, black and white oak, hickory, and ash.
	West, on a *true* line along the south boundary of section 32,
	Variation 18° 25′ east,
37.50	A creek, 20 links wide, runs north.
40.00	Set a granite stone, 14 in. long, 10 in. wide, and 4 in. thick, for quarter-section corner, from which
	A maple, 20 in. dia., bears N. 41 E., 25 links dist.;
	A birch, 24 in. dia., bears N. 35 W., 22 links dist.
76.00	To S. E. edge of swamp.
	As it is impossible to establish *permanently* the corner to sections 31, 32, 5, and 6 in the swamp, I therefore at this point, 400 chains east of the true point for said section cor., raise a witness mound with trench, as per instructions, from which
	A black oak, 20 in. dia., bears N. 51 E. 115 links.
80.00	A point in deep swamp for corner to sections 31, 32, 5, and 6.
	Land, rich bottom; *west* of creek part wet; *east* of creek good for farming.
	Timber, good; oak, hickory, and walnut.
	West, on a *true* line along the south boundary of section 31,
	Variation 18° 25′ east,
11.00	Leave swamp and rise bluff 30 feet high; bears N. and S.
40.00	Set post for quarter-section corner, from which
	A sugar tree, 27 in. dia., bears S. 81 W., 42 links dist.;
	A beech, 24 in. dia., bears S. 71 E. 24.
54.00	Foot of rocky bluff, 30 feet high; bears N. E. and S. W.
57.50	A spring branch comes out at the foot of the bluff 5 links wide; runs N. W. into swamp.
61.00	Enter swamp; bears N. and S.
70.00	Leave swamp; bears N. S. The swamp contains about 15 acres, the greater part in section 31.
74.73	The corner to townships 24 and 25 N., ranges 2 and 3 W.
	Land, except the swamp, rolling, good, rich soil.
	Timber, sugar tree, beech, and maple.
	January 25, 1854.

Between ranges 1 and 2 west, S. 25 N., Willamette meridian.
From the corner to townships 24 and 25 N., ranges 1 and 2 W., I run
North, along the east boundary of section 36,

34

Between ranges 1 *and* 2 *W.*, *T.* 25 *N.*, *Willamette meridian*—Continued.

Chains.	
	Variation 17° 51′ E.,
1.00	A brook 5 links wide, runs N. W.
18.00	To foot of hill, bearing N. W. and S. E.
20.00	To rocky bluff 50 feet high, bears N. W. and S. E.
40.00	Set a post for quarter-section corner, from which
	A beech 13 in. dia., bears N. 36 E., 22 links dist.;
	A poplar, 20 in. dia., bears S. 39 E., 42 links dist.
55.00	To top of rocky bluff 40 feet high; bears N. W. and S. E.
57.00	To foot of bluff, enter level, rich land.
72.50	A brook 10 links wide, runs N. W.
80.00	Set a post for corner to sections 25, 36, 30, and 31, from which
	A birch, 24 in. dia., bears N. 20 E., 49 links dist.;
	A sugar tree, 12 in. dia., bears N. 81 W., 25 links dist.:
	A white oak, 9 in. dia., bears S. 40 W., 60 links dist.;
	A poplar, 15 in. dia., bears S. 38 E., 12 links dist.
	Land, north and south parts rich and good for farming; middle part broken, 3d rate. Timber, beech, sugar tree, poplar, and white oak.
	North, on the east boundary of section 25,
	Variation 18° east,
5.51	A maple, 20 in. dia.
6.00	To foot of hill, rises moderately; bears E. and N. W.
40.00	Set quarter-section stone, (a rose quartz,) 15 inches long, 12 inches wide, and 3 inches thick, (on steep side hill, slopes west,) from which
	A poplar, 40 in. dia., bears N. 40 W., 10 links dist.;
	A beech, 9 in. dia., bears S. 42 W., 11 links dist.
73.21	A white oak, 20 in. dia.
80.00	Set a post for corner of sections 24, 25, 19, and 30, from which
	A beech, 20 in. dia., bears N. 64 E., 41 links dist.;
	A white oak, 10 in. dia., bears N. 30 W., 13 links dist.;
	A beech, 12 in. dia., bears S. 32 W., 26 links dist.;
	A white oak, 11 in. dia., bears S. 34 E., 48 links dist.
	Land rolling; good soil; nearly 1st rate.
	Timber, sugar tree, beech, walnut, elm, and white oak.
	North, on the east boundary of section 24,
	Variation 17° 55′ east,
21.17	A white walnut, 20 in. dia.
40.00	Set a quarter-section post, from which
	A buckeye, 14 in. dia., bears N. 39 E., 27 links dist.;
	A buckeye, 10 in. dia., bears S. 48 W., 6 links dist.
44.00	The road (at the foot of the bluff) from Williamsburg to Astoria, bears east and west.
49.00	Elk Creek, 150 links wide, gentle current, runs west.
57.10	A brook, 10 links wide, runs S. W.
59.67	A black oak, 24 in. dia.
65.50	Leave creek bottom and enter upland, bears E. and W.
80.00	Set a limestone, 16 in. long, 14 wide, and 3 in. thick, for corner to sections 13, 24, 18, and 19, from which
	A beech, 12 in. dia., bears N. 30 E., 50 links dist.;
	A walnut, 9 in. dia., bears N. 18 W., 29 links dist.:
	A walnut, 8 in. dia., bears S. 8 W., 51 links dist.;
	A beech, 6 in. dia., bears S. 20 E., 40 links dist.
	Land, except creek bottom, rolling; good rich soil. The bottom dry and rich, not subject to inundation.
	Timber, good; walnut, beech, maple, ash, and hickory.
	North, on the east boundary of section 13,
	Variation 17° 55′ east,
14.00	A white oak, 24 in. dia.
21.00	Enter high, broken ridges, bearing east and N. W.
40.00	Set a post for quarter-section corner, from which
	A cherry, 10 in. dia., bears N. 35 W., 2 links dist.;

Between ranges 1 *and* 2 *W., T.* 25 *N., Willamette meridian*—Continued.

Chains.	
43.71	A cherry, 10 in. dia., bears S. 52 E., 21 links dist.
80.00	A bur oak, 30 in. dia.
	Set a post for corner to sections 12, 13, 7 and 18, from which
	A hickory, 15 in. dia., bears N. 40 E., 14 links dist.;
	A hickory, 20 in. dia., bears N. 39 W., 38 links dist.;
	A beech, 12 in. dia., bears S. 36 W., 16 links dist.;
	A sugar tree, 10 in. dia., bears S. 42 E., 23 links dist.
	Land (except 21.00 chains, south part) high, broken, and mountainous.
	Timber, beech, hickory, sugar tree, and blackjack.
	North, on the east boundary of section 12,
	Variation 17° 55' east,
7.26	A black oak, 24 in. dia.
40.00	Set a post for quarter-section corner, from which
	A white ash, 10 in. dia., bears N. 35 W., 15 links dist.;
	An elm, 10 in. dia., bears S. 83 E., 2 links dist.
68.00	The foot of the mountain bears east and N. W.
80.00	Set a post on the top of eastern extremity of mountain, 300 feet high, for corner to sections 1, 12, 6 and 7, from which
	An elm, 12 in. dia., bears N. 46 E., 30 links dist.;
	A beech, 10 in. dia., bears N. 40 W., 28 links dist.;
	A hickory, 10 in. dia., bears S. 55 W., 40 links dist.;
	A beech, 10 in. dia., bears S. 40 E., 6 links dist.
	Land mountainous and broken.
	Timber, hickory, white oak, black oak, beech, and ash.
	North, on the east boundary of section 1,
	Variation 17° 55' east,
9.00	The foot of mountain bears east and west.
25.37	A white oak, 16 in. dia.
40.00	Set a post, in deep ravine bearing S. W., for quarter-section corner, from which
	A poplar, 9 in. dia., bears N. 76 E., 7 links dist.;
	A sugar tree, 9 in. dia., bears S. 22 E., 15 links dist.
44.00	Leave timber and enter prairie; bears E. and N. W.
80.00	To a point for corner to townships 25 and 26 N., ranges 1 and 2 W. Drove charred stake, and raised a mound with trench, as per instructions, and planted N. W. 4 chestnuts, S. W. 2 hickory nuts, N. E. 4 cherry stones, and S. E. 4 white-oak acorns.
	Land, south of prairie, mountainous and broken; prairie good for farming.
	Timber, sugar tree, cedar, and pine.
	January 26, 1854.
	From the corner to townships 24 and 25 N., ranges 2 and 3 west; I run North, on the range line between sections 31 and 36,
	Variation 18° 56' east,
8.56	Set a post on the left bank of Chickeeles River for corner to fractional sections 31 and 36, from which
	A hackberry, 11 in. dia., bears N. 50 E., 11 links dist.;
	A sycamore, 60 in. dia., bears S. 15 W., 24 links dist.
	I now cause a flag to be set on the *right* bank of the river, and in the line between sections 31 and 36. I now cross the river, and from a point on the right bank thereof, *west* of the corner just established on the left bank, I run *north*, on an offset line, 25 chains and 94 links, to a point 8 chains and 56 links *west* of the flag. I now set a post, in the place of the flag, for corner to fractional sections 31 and 36, from which
	A beech, 10 in. dia., bears N. 2 E., 12 links dist.;
	A black oak, 12 in. dia., bears N. 80 W., 16 links dist.
34.50	The corner above described.
40.00	Set a post for quarter-section corner, from which
	A bur oak, 20 in. dia., bears N. 37 E., 26 links dist.;
	A black oak, 24 in. dia., bears S. 75 W., 21 links dist.
43.41	A black walnut, 30 in. dia.

Between ranges 2 and 3 W., T. 25 N., Willamette meridian—Continued.

Chains.	

80.00	Set a post for corner to sections 30, 31, 25 and 36, from which
	    A beech, 14 in. dia., bears N. 20 E., 14 links dist.;
	    A hickory, 9 in. dia., bears N. 25 W., 12 links dist.;
	    A beech, 16 in. dia., bears S. 40 W., 16 links dist.;
	    A white oak, 10 in. dia., bears S. 44 E., 20 links dist.
	Land level; rich bottom; not subject to inundation.
	Timber, white and black oak, beech, hickory, and ash.

	North, between sections 25 and 30, Variation 18° 50' east,

27.73	Set a post, for corner to fractional sections 25 and 30, on the right bank of Chickeeles River, a navigable stream, which here runs S. E., from which
	    A willow, 6 in. dia., bears S. 37 W., 55 links dist.;
	    A maple, 20 in. dia., bears S. 30 E., 11 links dist.
	I now cause a flag to be set on the left bank of the river, and in the line between sections 25 and 30. From the above corner I run west 333 chains, to a point from which the flag bears N. 16° 30' E., which gives for the distance across the river on the line 11.27 chains; to which add 27.73, makes

39.00	To the flag on the bank. I here set a post for corner to fractional sections 25 and 30, from which
	    A hickory, 8 in. dia., bears N. 44 E., 17 links dist.;
	    A white oak, 8 in. dia., bears N. 15 W., 8 links dist.

40.00	Set a post for quarter-section corner, from which
	    A hickory, 9 in. dia., bears N. 16 E., 16 links dist.;
	    A buckeye, 10 in. dia., bears S. 16 E., 18 links dist.

43.71	A hickory, 24 in. dia.

80.00	Set a post for corner to sections 19, 30, 24, 25, from which
	    An elm, 6 in. dia., bears N. 82 E., 25 links dist.;
	    A sugar tree, 14 in. dia., bears N. 49 W., 4 links dist.;
	    An elm, 9 in. dia., bears S. 42 W., 30 links dist.;
	    A sugar tree, 10 in. dia., bears S. 55 E., 45 links dist.
	Land good; rich bottom; 1st rate.
	Timber, hickory, elm, buckeye, sugar tree, and ash.

	North, between sections 19 and 24, Variation 18° 50' east,

32.50	A hickory, 20 in. dia., on the left bank of Chickeeles River, marks it for corner to fractional sections 19 and 24, from which
	    A hackberry, 20 in. dia., bears S. 13 W., 27 links dist.;
	    A black oak, 24 in dia., bears S. 27 E., 31 links dist.
	I now cause a flag to be set on the right bank of the river, and in the line between sections 19 and 24, and from the corner run a *base* east 5.90 chains, to a point from which the flag bears N. 17 W.; continue the base east to a point 9.00 chains *east* of the corner of the river bank, from which the flag bears N. 25° 15' W., which gives, by calculation, as the mean result of the two observations, for the distance across the river, on the line between sections 19 and 24, 19.30 chains, to which add 32.50 chains, the distance to the river, makes

51.80	To the flag on the right bank of the river. I here set a post for corner to fractional sections 19 and 24, from which
	    A beech, 12 in. dia., bears N. 24 E. 39 links dist.;
	    A beech, 14 in. dia., bears S. 55 W., 120 links dist.
	NOTE.—The point for quarter-section corner falling in the river, it cannot, therefore, be established.

55.74	A black oak, 30 inches diameter.

80.00	Set a post for corner to sections 18, 19, 13, and 24, from which
	    A white oak, 18 in. dia., bears N. 55 E. 24 links dist.;
	    A white oak, 17 in. dia., bears N. 64 W., 18 links dist.;
	    A red oak, 27 in. dia., bears S. 26 W., 20 links dist.;
	    A red oak, 15 in. dia., bears S. 29 E., 40 links dist.
	Land good; rich bottom; not subject to inundation.
	Timber, various kinds of oak, beech, hickory, and ash; undergrowth, same and vines.

Between ranges 2 and 3 W., T. 25 N., Willamette meridian—Continued.

Chains.	
	North, between sections 13 and 18, Variation 18° 53' east,
5.00	Leave bottom and enter upland; bears N. E. and S. W.
21.88	A red oak, 20 in dia.
38.60	A white oak, 24 in. dia.
40.00	Set a post for quarter-section corner, from which A white oak, 22 in. dia., bears N. 27 W., 27 links dist.; A white oak, 23 in. dia., bears S. 28 E., 92 links dist.
46.50	A road from Williamsburg bears east and west.
68.37	A black walnut, 21 in. dia.
80.00	Set a post for corner to sections 7, 18, 12, and 13, from which A white oak, 12 in. dia., bears N. 55 E. 68 links dist.; A black oak, 8 in. dia., bears N. 53 W., 40 links dist.; A black oak, 16 in. dia., bears S. 40 W., 55 links dist.; A red oak, 10 in. dia., bears S. 44 E., 50 links dist.
	Land rolling, and next the bottom broken; soil 2d rate. Timber good; various kinds of oak and hickory.
	North, between sections 7 and 12, Variation 18° 53' east,
15.18	A white oak, 15 in. dia.
30.26	A white oak, 21 in. dia.
40.00	Set a post for quarter-section corner, from which A white oak, 12 in dia., bears S. 13 W., 60 links dist.; A white oak, 15 in dia., bears S. 35 E., 55 links dist.
68.37	A black walnut, 21 in. dia.
80.00	Set a post for corner to section 6, 7, 1, 12, from which A white oak, 17 in. dia., bears N. 58 E., 60 links dist.; A white oak, 18 in. dia., bears N. 54 W., 51 links dist.; A white oak, 18 in. dia., bears S. 51 W., 20 links dist.; A hickory, 14 in. dia., bears S. 64 E., 42 links dist.
	Land gently rolling; 2d rate. Timber, oak and hickory; undergrowth, oak and hazel.
	North, between sections 1 and 6, Variation 18° 53' east.
3.00	Enter *stony* barrens; timber scattering; bears E. and W.
25.31	A blackjack, 12 in. dia.
40.00	Set a quartz stone, 13 in. long, 12 in. wide, and 4 in. thick, for quarter-section corner, with trench, as per instructions, from which A blackjack, 20 in. dia., bears S. 44 E., 95 links dist. No other tree convenient to mark.
45.00	Leave *stony* barrens; bears E. and W.
61.11	A hickory, 10 in. dia. Here leave timber and enter prairie, bearing W. and N. E.
80.00	Set a granite stone 18 in. long, 12 in. wide, and 6 in. thick, for corner to townships 25 and 26 north, ranges 2 and 3 west; raise a stone mound, with trench, as per instructions.
	Land broken and stony; too poor for cultivation. Timber, scattering and poor; blackjack and hickory.
	January 27, 1851.

From the corner to townships 25 and 26 N., ranges 2 and 3 west, I run East, on a *random* line between said townships, the variation of my compass being 18° 41' E., I set temporary half-mile and mile posts at 40.00 and 80.00 chains.
At 160.09 intersected the right bank of Chickeeles River, a navigable stream, where set a temporary post; obtain the distance across the river on the line by causing my flag to be set on the left bank of the river, in said line.
From the temporary post on the right bank, I run north, 7 chains 63 links to a point, thence east, on an offset line, and at 30.00 chains, a point north of the flag standing on the left bank of the river, set a temporary post in the place of the flag.

Between townships 25 and 26 N., R. 2 W., Willamette meridian—Cont'd.

Chains.	
	I find the township line to be 5 miles 76 chains 53 links, and the falling to be 25 links north of the township corner. The correction for the true line will therefore be 3 chains 47 links west and 4.2 links south per mile.

	From the corner to townships 25 and 26 north, ranges 1 and 2 west, I run West, on a *true* line between sections 1 and 36, Variation 18° 39' east,
20.00	Leave prairie and enter scattering timber; bears N. and S.
40.00	Set a post for quarter-section corner, from which
	A beech, 24 in. dia., bears N. 11 E., 38 links dist.;
	A beech, 9 in. dia., bears S. 9 W., 19 links dist.
43.71	A black walnut, 30 in. dia.
80.00	Set a sandstone, 16 in. long, 12 in. wide, and 3 in. thick, for corner to sections 1, 2, 35, and 36, from which
	A buckeye, 9 in dia., bears N. 66 E., 15 links dist.;
	An elm, 20 in. dia., bears N. 4 W., 10 links dist.;
	An elm, 36 in. dia., bears S. 65 W., 8 links dist.;
	A buckeye, 10 in. dia., bears S. 40 E., 20 links dist.
	Land level, or gently rolling, and 1st rate.
	Timber, scattering next the prairies; elm, buckeye, beech, walnut, and oak.

	West, on a *true* line between sections 2 and 35, Variation 18° 39' east,
27.13	A white oak, 24 in. dia.
40.00	Set a post for quarter-section corner, from which
	A white oak, 9 in. dia., bears N. 24 E., 28 links dist.;
	A buckeye, 12 in. dia., bears S. 48 W., 9 links dist.
75.59	A black oak, 24 in. dia.
80.00	Set a post for corner to sections 2, 3, 34, and 35, from which
	A sugar tree, 15 in. dia., bears N. 46 E., 15 links dist.
	No tree convenient in section 34.
	A beech, 16 in. dia., bears S. 35 W., 16 links dist.;
	A sugar tree, 14 in. dia., bears S. 30 E., 14 links dist.
	Land gently rolling, and 1st rate.
	Timber, good; elm, buckeye, beech, walnut, and oak.

	West, on a *true* line between sections 3 and 34, Variation 18° 39' east.
9.00	Enter wet prairie; bears N. and S.
16.00	A beautiful spring branch, 5 links wide, runs S. W.
22.00	Leave prairie; bears N. E. and S. W.
31.27	A black oak, 20 in. dia.
40.00	Set a post for quarter-section corner from which
	A white walnut, 16 in. dia., bears N. 64 E., 7 links dist.;
	A white walnut, 12 in. dia., bears S. 73 W., 31 links dist.
41.33	A white oak, 30 in. dia.
74.52	A point 4 links south of a black oak, 24 in. dia.; mark it by cutting 2 notches south side.
75.00	Leave timber and enter a narrow strip of prairie; bears N. W. and S. E.
80.00	A point for corner to sections 3, 4, 33, and 34, drove a charred stake, and raised a mound, with trench, as per instructions, from which
	A white oak, 20 in. dia., bears N. 73 E., 540 links dist.;
	A black oak, 30 in. dia., bears S. 76 E., 613 links dist.
	Land gently rolling; 1st rate.
	Timber, white and black oak, walnut, and sugar tree.

	West, on a *true* line between sections 4 and 33, Variation 18° 39' east.
7.50	Leave prairie; bears N. W. and S. E.
21.50	A spring branch, 15 links wide, runs N. W.
40.00	A black walnut, 30 in. dia.; mark it for quarter-section corner, from which

39

Between townships 25 and 26 N., R. 2 W., Willamette meridian—Cont'd.

Chains.	
	A buckeye, 9 in. dia., bears S. 45 E., 11 links dist.;
	A black walnut, 20 in. dia., bears N. 29 W., 25 links dist.
41.40	Leave upland and enter river bottom; bears N. E. and S. W.
46.44	Set a post on the left bank of Chickeeles River, for corner to fractional sections 4 and 33, from which
	An elm, 8 in. dia., bears N. 71 E., 5 links dist.;
	An elm, 10 in. dia., bears S. 19 W., 6 links dist.
	The line running in the river, the distance on the *random* line was obtained on an offset by running *north* from the temporary post on the right bank 7 chains 63 links to a point thence *east* 30.00 chains, and coming back to *true* line on the left bank of the river.
76.44	Set a post on the right bank of the river for corner to fractional sections 4 and 33, from which
	A cherry, 6 in. dia., bears N. 61 E., 17 links dist.;
	A sugar tree, 20 in. dia., bears S. 75 W., 20 links dist.
76.64	A sugar tree, 23 in. dia.
80.00	Set a post for corner to sections 4, 5, 32, and 33, from which
	A hackberry, 7 in. dia., bears N. 67 E., 17 links dist.;
	A sugar tree, 20 in. dia., bears N. 71 W., 43 links dist.;
	A locust, 14 in. dia., bears S. 30 W., 16 links dist.;
	A beech, 20 in. dia., bears S. 20 E., 50 links dist.
	Land, east of bottom, rolling; good soil; the bottom subject to inundation 4 feet.
	Timber, on upland, oak; in bottom, sugar, cherry, and hackberry.

	West, on a *true* line between sections 5 and 32,
	Variation 18° 39′ east,
24.40	A white oak, 16 in. dia. Here leave bottom and enter hills; bears N. E. and S. W.
40.00	Set a post for quarter-section corner, from which
	A hickory, 18 in. dia., bears N. 88 E., 40 links dist.;
	A mulberry, 14 in. dia., bears S. 69 W., 103 links dist.
42.73	A black ash, 15 in. dia.
80.00	Set a post for corner to sections 5, 6, 31, and 32, from which
	A sugar tree, 20 in. dia., bears N. 89 E., 60 links dist.;
	An elm, 14 in. dia., bears N. 12 W., 24 links dist.;
	An elm, 15 in. dia., bears S. 14 W., 23 links dist.;
	A sugar tree, 16 in. dia., bears S. 15 E., 26 links dist.
	Land gently rolling, and 1st rate; the bottom level.
	Timber, sugar tree, walnut, and oak; undergrowth same, and spice.

	West, on a *true* line between sections 6 and 31,
	Variation 18° 39′ east,
8.00	To swamp of about 15 acres; bears N. E. and S. W.
18.00	Leave swamp; bears N. E. and S. W.; the line passes through the middle of the swamp.
18.26	A red oak, 30 in. dia., on N. W. bank of swamp.
34.30	A hickory, 18 in. dia.
40.00	Set a post for quarter-section corner, from which
	A bur oak, 27 in. dia., bears N. 49 E., 46 links dist.;
	A sugar tree, 20 in. dia., bears N. 56 W., 60 links dist.
	No tree convenient *south* of the line.
48.65	A stream, 14 links wide, runs south.
57.40	A white oak, 28 in. dia.
61.00	Enter prairie; bears N. E. and S. W.
76.53	To the established corner to townships 25 and 26 N., ranges 2 and 3 west.
	Land level; 1st rate for farming.
	Timber, good; various kinds of oak, hickory, and sugar tree; undergrowth, hazel, hickory, and vines.

GENERAL DESCRIPTION.

This township contains a large amount of first-rate land for farming. It is well timbered with the various kinds of oak, hickory, sugar tree, walnut, beech, and ash.

Chickeeles River is navigable for small boats in low water, and does not often overflow its banks, which are from ten to fifteen feet high.

The township will admit of a large settlement, and should therefore be subdivided.

B.

FIELD-NOTES OF THE SUBDIVISION LINES AND MEANDERS OF CHICK-EELES RIVER, IN TOWNSHIP 25 NORTH, RANGE 2 WEST, WILLAMETTE MERIDIAN.

Township 25 N., range 2 W., Willamette meridian.

Chains.	
	To determine the proper adjustment of my compass for subdividing this township, I commence at the corner to townships 24 and 25 N., R. 1 and 2 W., and run
	North, on a blank line along the east boundary of section 36,
	Variation 17° 51′ east,
40.05	To a point 5 links west of the quarter-section corner.
80.09	To a point 12 links west of the corner to sections 25 and 36.
	To retrace this line or run parallel thereto, my compass must be adjusted to a variation of 17° 46′ east.
	Subdivision commenced February 1, 1854.
	From the corner to sections 1, 2, 35, and 36, on the south boundary of the township, I run
	North, between sections 35 and 36,
	Variation 17° 46′ east,
9.19	A beech, 30 in. dia.
29.97	A beech, 30 in. dia.
40.00	Set a post for quarter-section corner, from which
	A beech, 8 in. dia., bears N. 23 W., 45 links dist.;
	A beech, 15 in. dia., bears S. 48 E., 12 links dist.
51.00	A beech, 18 in. dia.
76.00	A sugar tree, 30 in. dia.
80.00	Set a post for corner to sections 25, 26, 35, and 36, from which
	A beech, 28 in. dia., bears N. 60 E., 45 links dist.;
	A beech, 24 in. dia., bears N. 62 W., 17 links dist.;
	A poplar, 20 in. dia., bears S. 70 W., 50 links dist.;
	A poplar, 36 in. dia., bears S. 66 E., 34 links dist.
	Land level; 2d rate.
	Timber, poplar, beech, sugar tree, and some oak; undergrowth, same and hazel.
	East, on a *random* line between sections 25 and 36,
	Variation 17° 46′ east,
9.00	A brook, 20 links wide, runs north.
15.00	To foot of hills, bear N. and S.
40.00	Set a post for temporary quarter-section corner.
55.00	To opposite foot of hill, bears N. and S.
72.00	A brook, 15 links wide, runs north.
80.00	Intersected east boundary at post corner to sections 25 and 36, from which corner I run
	West, on a *true* line between sections 25 and 36,
	Variation 17° 46′ east,
40.00	Set a post on top of hill, bears N. and S., from which
	A hickory, 14 in. dia., bears N. 60 E., 27 links dist.;
	A beech, 15 in. dia., bears S. 74 W., 9 links dist.
80.00	The corner to sections 25 and 26, 35 and 36.
	Land, east and west parts, level, 1st rate; middle part broken, 3d rate.
	Timber, beech, oak, ash, &c.; undergrowth, same and spice in the branch bottoms.
	North, between sections 25 and 26,
	Variation 17° 46′ east,
7.00	A poplar, 40 in. dia.
17.20	A brook, 25 links wide, runs N. W.

Township 25 N., range 2 W., Willamette meridian—Continued.

Chains.	
18.05	A walnut, 30 in. dia.
23.44	A brook, 25 links wide, runs N. E.
40.00	Set a post for quarter-section corner, from which
	A bur oak, 36 in. dia., bears N. 42 E., 18 links dist.;
	A beech, 30 in. dia., bears S. 72 W., 9 links dist.
60.15	A beech, 30 in. dia.
80.00	Set a post for corner to sections 23, 24, 25, and 26, from which
	A white oak, 14 in. dia., bears N. 50 E. 40 links;
	A sugar tree, 12 in. dia., bears N. 14 W., 31 links dist.;
	A white oak, 13 in. dia., bears S. 38 W., 32 links dist.;
	A sugar tree, 12 in. dia., bears S. 42 E., 14 links dist.
	Land level on the line, high ridge of hills through the middle of section 25 running N. and S.
	Timber, beech, walnut, ash, sugar tree, &c.

East, on a *random* line between sections 24 and 25,
Variation 17° 46' east.

8.90	A stream, 30 links wide, rapid current, runs N. W.
12.00	To foot of hill, bears south and N. E.
40.00	Set a post for temporary quarter-section corner.
48.00	To opposite foot of hill, bears south and N. W.
60.50	A stream, 30 links wide, runs N.; soon turns N. W.
73.00	To foot of hill, rises moderately, bears S. and N. W.
80.12	Intersected east boundary of the township at the post corner to sections 24 and 25, from which corner I run

West, on a *true* line between sections 24 and 25.
Variation 17° 46' east.

40.06	Set a post for quarter-section corner, from which
	A beech, 18 in. dia., bears N. 74 W., 26 links dist.;
	A beech, 16 in. dia., bears S. 73 E., 22 links dist.
80.12	The corner to sections 23, 24, 25, 26.
	Land rolling between the branches; good, 2d rate; branch bottoms level, 1st rate.
	Timber, walnut, beech, elm, and oak; undergrowth, same and spice.

North, between sections 23 and 24,
Variation 17° 46' east.

6.70	A white oak, 20 in. dia.
9.65	A stream, 15 links wide, runs N. W.
13.50	Same stream, 25 links wide, runs N. E.
16.00	Same stream, 25 links wide, runs N. W.
40.00	Set a post near the south bank of a stream for quarter-section corner, from which
	A cottonwood, 18 in. dia., bears S. 7 W., 7 links dist.;
	A white walnut, 24 in. dia., bears S. 22 E., 4 links dist.
40.35	Elk Creek, 125 links wide, runs N. W.; general course, west.
	John Jones has a field on the north side of the creek and west of the line; his house is 2 chains south of the road and 2 chains east of the line.
54.00	To the road from Astoria to Williamsburg; bears E. and W.
58.00	Enter wet prairie; bears east and west.
68.00	Leave prairie and enter timber bearing east and west.
	This prairie extends *east* into section 24 about 30 chains.
75.12	A white oak, 30 in. dia.
75.00	Leave creek bottom and enter hills bearing east and west.
80.00	Set a post for corner to sections 13, 14, 23, 24, from which
	A white walnut, 16 in. dia., bears N. 42 E., 15 links dist.;
	A white walnut, 24 in. dia., bears N. 59 W., 27 links dist.;
	An elm, 8 in. dia., bears S. 67 W., 16 links dist.;
	A black oak, 14 in. dia., bears S. 38 E., 17 links dist.
	Land mostly level; 1st rate soil.
	Timber, walnut, various kinds of oak, buckeye, and hickory; undergrowth, same and spice.

February 1, 1854.

Township 25 N., range 2 W., Willamette meridian—Continued.

Chains.	
	East, on a *random* line between sections 13 and 24, Variation 17° 46' east,
40.00	Set a post for temporary quarter-section corner.
80.10	Intersected the east boundary of township, 16 links south of post corner, to sections 13 and 24, from which corner I run West, on a *true* line between sections 13 and 24, Variation 17° 53' east,
40.05	Set a post for quarter-section corner, from which A sugar tree, 30 in. dia., bears N. 80 W., 22 links dist.; A white oak, 16 in. dia., bears S. 53 E., 20 links dist.
80.10	The corner to sections 13, 14, 23, 24. Land mostly rolling; good rich soil; 1st rate. Timber, walnut, sugar tree, oak, elm, and buckeye; undergrowth, same and spice.
	North, between sections 13 and 14, Variation 17° 46' east,
6.17	A white oak, 30 in. dia.
22.15	A beech, 30 in. dia.
40.00	Set a post for quarter-section corner, from which A beech, 24 in. dia., bears N. 66 W., 6 links dist.; A beech, 20 in. dia., bears S. 45 E., 40 links dist.
52.25	A beech, 24 in. dia.
62.61	A bur oak, 30 in. dia.
80.00	Set a post for corner to sections 11, 12, 13, 14, from which A black oak, 26 in. dia., bears N. 53 E., 10 links dist.; A black oak, 21 in. dia., bears N. 20 W., 35 links dist.; A sugar tree, 30 in. dia., bears S. 32 W., 25 links dist.; A white oak, 20 in. dia., bears S. 24 E., 20 links dist. Land gently rolling; good, 2d rate. Timber, beech, oak, and ash; undergrowth, same and hazel.
	East, on a *random* line between sections 12 and 13, Variation 17° 46' east,
20.50	Foot of hills, and enter broken ridges bearing north and south.
40.00	Set a post for temporary quarter-section corner.
80.10	Intersected east boundary 13 links north of post corner to sections 12 and 13, from which corner I run West, on a *true* line between sections 12 and 13, Variation 17° 40' east,
40.05	Set a post for quarter-section corner, from which An elm, 24 in. dia., bears N. 51 E., 50 links dist.; A beech, 18 in. dia., bears S. 51 W., 29 links dist.
80.10	The corner to sections 11, 12, 13, 14. Land west 20 chains; gently rolling; good, 2d rate; the balance high, broken ridges. Timber, beech, black oak, and white oak; undergrowth, same and hazel.
	North, between sections 11 and 12, Variation 17° 46' east,
10.81	An elm, 15 in. dia.
40.00	Set a post for quarter-section corner, from which A beech, 30 in. dia., bears N. 33 W., 9 links dist.; A beech, 20 in. dia., bears S. 64 W., 20 links dist.
52.25	A beech, 24 in. dia.
62.61	A black oak, 30 in. dia.
75.40	A spring branch, 10 links wide, runs west.
80.00	Set a post for corner to sections 1, 2, 11, and 12, from which A poplar, 32 in. dia., bears N. 41 E., 30 links dist.; A poplar, 36 in. dia., bears N. 43 W., 25 links dist.; A sugar tree, 30 in. dia., bears S. 32 W., 25 links dist.; A sugar tree, 21 in. dia., bears S. 35 E., 40 links dist. Land level; good, 2d rate. Timber, sugar tree, poplar, walnut, and oak; undergrowth, same and hazel.

Township 25 N., range 2 W., Willamette meridian—Continued.

Chains.	
	East, on a *random* line between sections 1 and 12, Variation 17° 46' east,
23.00	Enter high, broken ridges, bearing N. E. and south.
40.00	Set a post for temporary quarter-section corner.
42.50	A spring branch, 10 links wide, runs S. W.
63.00	To foot of high mountain; bears north and south.
80.24	Intersected the east boundary of the township 13 links north of post corner to sections 1 and 12, from which corner I run West, on a *true* line between sections 1 and 12, Variation 17° 40' east,
40.12	Set a post on top of narrow ridge, bearing north and south, for quarter-section corner, from which A sugar tree, 20 in. dia., bears N. 20 E., 32 links dist.; A sugar tree, 24 in. dia., bears S. 56 W., 25 links dist.
80.24	The corner to sections 1, 2, 11, 12. Land very broken and mountainous. Timber, sugar tree, beech; various kinds of oak and hickory. ☞On this line, and toward the foot of the mountain, we discovered gold dust; and throughout the line we observed many specimens of what appeared to be rich auriferous quartz.
	North, on a *random* line between sections 1 and 2, Variation 17° 46' east,
40.00	Set a post for temporary quarter-section corner.
80.11	Intersected the north boundary 32 links east of corner to sections 1 and 2, from which corner I run South, on a *true* line between sections 1 and 2, Variation 18° 00' east,
40.11	Set a post for quarter-section corner, from which A white oak, 20 in. dia., bears N. 31 W., 65 links dist.; A sugar tree, 14 in. dia., bears S. 49 E., 32 links dist.
80.11	The corner to sections 1, 2, 11, 12. Land level; good, rich, soil. Timber, walnut, sugar tree, beech, and various kinds of oak; open woods.
	February 2, 1854.
	North, between sections 34 and 35, Variation 17° 46' east,
6.56	A hickory, 36 in. dia.
23.00	To foot of hill; bears east and west.
34.58	A walnut, 38 in. dia.
40.00	Set a post for quarter-section corner, from which A beech, 16 in. dia., bears S. 18 E., 13 links dist.; A beech, 10 in. dia., bears N. 69 W., 40 links dist.
50.00	A maple, 24 in. dia.
75.86	An ash, 24 in. dia.
80.00	Set a post for corner to sections 26, 27, 34, and 35, from which An ash, 30 in. dia., bears N. 30 E., 24 links dist.; An ash, 36 in. dia., bears N. 52 W., 19 links dist.; A beech, 16 in. dia., bears S. 69 W., 41 links dist.; A beech, 14 in. dia., bears S. 67 E., 12 links dist. Land, south 23 chains, broken; the balance level, rich soil. Timber, ash, beech, oak, and hickory; undergrowth, same and spice.
	East, on a *random* line between sections 26 and 35, Variation 17° 46' east,
40.00	Set a post for temporary quarter-section corner.
80.08	Intersected N. and S. line 20 links north of the corner to sections 25, 26, 35, and 36, from which corner I run West, on a *true* line between sections 26 and 35, Variation 17° 37' east,
40.04	Set a post for quarter-section corner, from which A beech, 14 in. dia., bears N. 56 E., 12 links dist.;

Township 25 N., range 2 W., Willamette meridian—Continued.

Chains.	
80.08	A beech, 12 in. dia., bears S. 32 W., 32 links dist. The corner to sections 26, 27, 34, and 35. Land level; good, rich soil. Timber, beech, elm, ash, and walnut.

North, between sections 26 and 27,
Variation 17° 46' east,

8.47	An elm, 20 in. dia.;
29.18	A lynn, 34 in. dia.
40.00	Set a post for quarter-section corner, from which A sugar tree, 14 in. dia., bears N. 54 E., 27 links dist.; A beech, 12 in. dia., bears S. 13 W., 31 links dist.
46.37	A poplar, 40 in. dia.;
60.48	A black oak, 36 in. dia.
80.00	Set a post for corner to sections 22, 23, 26, 27, from which A white oak, 30 in. dia., bears N. 50 E., 13 links dist.; A walnut, 30 in. dia., bears N. 36 W., 14 links dist.; A walnut, 24 in. dia., bears S. 24 W., 16 links dist.; An ironwood, 8 in. dia., bears S. 32 E., 24 links dist. Land, south half, 2d rate; north half, 1st rate. Timber, walnut, poplar, white oak, beech, and hickory. ☞About 10 chains from this corner on the S. W., and on the left bank of Elk Creek, we discovered evidences of extensive ancient works, supposed to be fortifications, with many ancient mounds in the vicinity.

East, on a *random* line between sections 23 and 26,
Variation 17° 46' east,

40.00	Set a post for temporary quarter-section corner.
48.00	A stream, 12 links wide, outlet to a lake in the middle of section 26, runs N. W.
80.00	Intersected north and south line 15 links north of post corner to sections 23, 24, 25, 26, from which corner I run West, on a *true* line between sections 23 and 26, Variation 17° 40' east,
40.00	Set a post for quarter-section corner, from which A beech, 16 in. dia., bears N. 72 W., 18 links dist.; A beech, 10 in. dia., bears S. 72 W., 16 links dist.
80.00	The corner to sections 22, 23, 26, 27. Land level, good; 2d rate soil. Timber, beech, sugar tree, elm, and hickory.

Notes of the meanders of a small lake in section 26.

Begin at the quarter-section corner on the line between sections 23 and 26, and run thence south,

| 24.00 | To the north margin of the lake, where set a post for meander corner, from which
A beech, 14 in. dia., bears N. 45 E., 10 links dist.;
A beech, 9 in. dia., bears N. 15 W., 14 links dist.
Thence meander around the lake as follows:
S. 53° E., 17.75. At 75 links cross outlet to lake, 10 links wide, runs N. E.
S. 3° E., 13.00,
S. 30' W., 8.00,
S. 65° W., 12.00, to a point previously determined 20.30 chains *north* of the quarter-section corner, on the line between sections 26 and 35,
Set post meander corner, maple, 16 in. dia., bears S. 15 W., 20 links dist.
Ash, 12 in dia., bears S. 21 E., 15 links dist.
N. 63° W., 10.00. ⎫ In this vicinity we discovered remarkable fossil remains
N. 13° W., 21.00. ⎬ of animals well worthy the attention of naturalists.
N. 52° E., 17.30, to the place of beginning.
This is a beautiful lake, with well-defined banks from 6 to 10 feet high.
Land, 1st rate. |

Township 25 N., range 2 W., Willamette meridian—Continued.

Chains.	
	North, between sections 22 and 23, Variation 17° 46′ east,
8.00	Elk Creek, 150 links wide, runs S. W.
24.20	Same creek, rapid current, rocky bed and banks, 150 links wide, runs S. E.

40.00	Set a post for quarter-section corner, from which
	     A black oak, 20 in. dia., bears N. 34 E. 48 links;
	     A black oak, 20 in. dia., bears S. 9 W. 45 links.

41.60	Same creek, 150 links wide, rocky bed and banks, runs west. About 500 chains below the crossing of the line, a stream 20 links wide comes in from the north. Two chains below the mouth of this stream the creek turns south. Here is a very fine mill seat, the fall in the river being about 6 feet in the distance of three chains. Both banks of the creek about 10 feet high, composed principally of limestone of excellent quality.
47.00	Enter wet prairie near the west end, bearing N. W. and east.
65.00	Leave wet prairie, bearing east and west.
68.00	The road from Astoria to Williamsburg, bearing S. 80 E., and N. 60 W.
69.92	A white oak, 18 in. dia.
70.50	Enter high, rolling land, bearing east and west.

80.00	Set a post for corner to sections 14, 15, 22, and 23, from which
	     An elm, 16 in. dia., bears N. 27 E., 50 links dist.;
	     An elm, 24 in. dia., bears N. 34 W., 45 links dist.;
	     A sugar tree, 18 in. dia., bears S. 60 W., 42 links dist.;
	     A sugar tree, 24 in. dia., bears S. 52 E., 23 links dist.

	Land, south of wet prairie at 47 chains, broken, 3d rate; the balance part wet, 2d rate.
	Timber, elm, sugar tree, oak, and hickory.
	February 3, 1854.
	East, on a *random* line between sections 14 and 23, Variation 17° 46′ east,
40.00	Set a post for temporary quarter-section corner.
80.14	Intersected north and south line 14 links north of the corner to sections 13, 14, 23, and 24, from which corner I run
	West, on a *true* line between sections 14 and 23, Variation 17° 40′ east,

40.07	Set a post for quarter-section corner, from which
	     A sugar tree, 30 in. dia., bears N. 39 E., 31 links dist.;
	     A mulberry, 12 in. dia., bears S. 26 W., 4 links dist.

80.14	To corner to sections 14, 15, 22, 23.
	Land gently rolling; good soil.
	Timber, elm, sugar tree, oak, and mulberry.
	North, between sections 14 and 15, Variation 17° 46′ east,
14.14	A sugar tree, 14 in. dia.
34.13	A white oak, 22 in. dia.

40.00	Set a post for quarter-section corner, from which
	     A beech, 24 in. dia., bears N. 45 W., 37 links dist.;
	     A sugar tree, 20 in. dia., bears S. 43 E., 74 links dist.

47.20	A walnut, 27 in. dia.
61.84	A white oak, 36 in. dia.
77.72	A stream, 25 links wide, rapid current, runs S. W.

80.00	Set a post for corner to sections 10, 11, 14, 15, from which
	     A bur oak, 28 in. dia., bears N. 16 E., 40 links dist.;
	     A black oak, 30 in. dia., bears N. 17 W., 32 links dist.;
	     A white oak, 14 in. dia., bears S. 15 W., 38 links dist.;
	     A hickory, 15 in. dia., bears S. 12 E. 36.

	Land gently rolling; 2d rate.
	Timber, various kinds of oak, beech, and walnut; open woods.
	East, on a *random* line between sections 11 and 14, Variation 17° 46′ east,
8.25	A stream, 25 links wide, runs S. W.

46

Township 25 N., range 2 W., Willamette meridian—Continued.

Chains.	
13.00	A stream, 10 links wide, runs N. W.
40.00	Set a post for temporary quarter-section corner.
80.16	Intersected N. and S. line 20 links north of post corner to sections 11, 12, 13, 14, from which corner I run
	West, on a *true* line between sections 11 and 14,
	Variation 17° 37' east,
40.08	Set a post for quarter-section corner, from which
	A sugar tree, 16 in. dia., bears N. 66 E., 35 links dist.;
	A sugar tree, 14 in. dia., bears S. 44 W., 13 links dist.
80.16	To corner to sections 10, 11, 14, 15.
	Land rolling, but not broken; good soil.
	Timber, good; various kinds of oak, beech, sugar tree, elm, and ash.

	North, between sections 10 and 11,
	Variation 17° 40' east,
5.29	A white oak, 24 in. dia.
39.16	A white oak, 36 in. dia.
40.00	Set a post for quarter-section corner, from which
	A beech, 15 in. dia., bears N. 18 W., 42 links dist.;
	A beech, 18 in. dia., bears S. 62 E., 12 links dist.
45.17	A sugar tree, 27 in. dia.
63.79	A sugar tree, 30 in. dia.
71.12	A brook, 20 links wide, rapid current, gravelly bottom, runs west; soon turns south.
80.00	Set a post for corner to sections 2, 3, 10, 11, from which
	A sugar tree, 18 in. dia., bears N. 13 E., 61 links dist.;
	A beech, 24 in. dia., bears N. 48 W., 26 links dist.;
	A white oak, 13 in. dia., bears S. 39 W., 40 links dist.
	No tree in section 11 convenient to mark.
	Land gently rolling, good, 2d rate.
	Timber, various kinds of oak, beech, walnut; open woods.

	East, on a *random* line between sections 2 and 11,
	Variation 17° 40' east,
18.36	A brook, 20 links wide, runs S. W.
40.00	Set a post for temporary quarter-section corner.
80.10	Intersected N. and S. line 12 links north of the corner to sections 1, 2, 11, 12, from which corner I run
	West, on a *true* line between sections 2 and 11,
	Variation 17° 35' east,
40.05	Set a post for quarter-section corner, from which
	A beech, 18 in. dia., bears N. 35 W., 5 links dist.;
	A beech, 14 in. dia., bears S. 47 E., 49 links dist.
80.10	The corner to sections 2, 3, 10, 11.
	Land gently rolling; soil good.
	Timber, beech, sugar tree, elm, and oak; west part brushy; east part open woods.

	North, on a *random* line between sections 2 and 3,
	Variation 17° 40' east,
40.00	Set a post for temporary quarter-section corner.
80.00	Intersected the north boundary of the township 25 links east of the corner to sections 2 and 3, from which corner I run
	South, on a *true* line between sections 2 and 3,
	Variation 17° 51' east,
40.00	Set a post for quarter-section corner, from which
	An elm, 8 in. dia., bears N. 35 W., 5 links dist.;
	A hickory, 10 in. dia., bears S. 75 E., 18 links dist.
80.00	The corner to sections 2, 3, 10, 11.
	Land gently rolling; good, 2d rate.
	Timber, various kinds of oak, beech, elm, and hickory; open woods.
	February 4, 1854.

Township 25 *N., range* 2 *W., Willamette meridian*—Continued.

Chains.	
	North, between sections 33 and 34,
	Variation 17° 46′ east,
5.61	An ash, 22 in. dia.
13.20	An elm, 15 in. dia.
40.00	Set a sand stone, 15 in. long, 12 in. wide, and 4 in. thick, for quarter-section corner, from which
	A beech, 15 in. dia., bears N. 22 E., 22 links dist.;
	A beech, 24 in. dia., bears S. 78 W., 15 links dist.
49.10	A black oak, 36 in. dia.
71.04	An elm, 30 in. dia.
80.00	Set a post on high ridge bearing N. S. for corner to sections 27, 28, 33, 34, from which
	A white oak, 14 in. dia., bears N. 22 E., 18 links dist.;
	A beech, 8 in. dia., bears N. 48 W., 14 links dist.;
	An elm, 12 in. dia., bears S. 16 W., 42 links dist.;
	A beech, 10 in. dia., bears S. 74 E., 14 links dist.
	Land broken, poor soil, not fit for cultivation.
	Timber, beech, oak, sugar tree, and elm.
	East, on a *random* line between sections 27 and 34,
	Variation 17° 46′ east,
18.00	To foot of hill bearing north and S. E.
40.00	Set a post for temporary quarter-section corner.
48.20	A brook, 20 links wide, runs north.
50.20	A brook, 15 links wide, runs N. W.
79.90	Intersected N. and S. line 14 links north of the corner to sections 26, 27, 34. and 35, from which corner I run
	West, on a *true* line between sections 27 and 34.
	Variation 17° 40′ east,
39.95	Set a post for quarter-section corner, from which
	A sugar tree, 15 in. dia., bears N. 32 W., 32 links dist.;
	A sugar tree, 15 in. dia., bears S. 52 E., 26 links dist.
79.90	The corners to sections 27, 28, 33, and 34.
	Land east of hill gently rolling; good soil.
	Timber, sugar tree, elm, oak, and ash.
	North, between sections 27 and 28.
	Variation 17° 46′ east,
2.11	A black oak, 30 in. dia.
20.42	An elm, 36 in. dia.
34.00	To foot of hill bearing S. W. and S. E.
40.00	Set a post for quarter-section corner, from which
	A buckeye, 10 in dia., bears N. 30 W., 6 links dist.;
	A poplar, 36 in. dia., bears S. 15 E., 38 links dist.
62.16	A sugar tree, 24 in. dia.
64.20	Elk Creek, 200 links wide, rapid current; bluff bank 20 feet high; south side runs west; enter bottom after crossing creek.
80.00	Set a sandstone, 16 in. long, 12 in. wide, and 6 in. thick, for corner to sections 21, 22, 27, 28, from which
	An elm, 15 in. dia., bears N. 31 E., 14 links dist.;
	A beech, 14 in. dia., bears N. 43 W., 37 links dist.;
	An elm, 20 in. dia., bears S..24 W., 24 links dist.;
	A beech, 24 in. dia., bears S. 20 E., 52 links dist.
	Land, south of creek, broken and rolling, 3d rate; north of creek rich bottom.
	Timber, beech, elm, various kinds of oak and hickory.
	East, on a *random* line between sections 22 and 27.
	Variation 17° 46′ east,
40.00	Set a post for temporary quarter-section corner.
75 70	Elk Creek, 200 links wide, gentle current, gravelly bottom, runs S. W.
80.06	Intersected north and south line 15 links north of the corner to sections 22, 23, 26, and 27, from which corner I run
	West, on a *true* line between sections 22 and 27,

48

Township 25 N., range 2 W., Willamette meridian—Continued.

Chains.	
40.03	Variation 17° 40' east,
	Set a post for quarter-section corner, from which
	An elm, 14 in. dia., bears N. 50 E., 16 links dist.;
	A mulberry, 10 in dia., bears S. 87 W., 43 links dist.
80.06	The corner to sections 21, 22, 27, 28.
	Land level; rich bottom; 2d rate.
	Timber, elm, beech, oak, and hickory.
	North, between sections 21 and 22,
	Variation 17° 46' east,
3.15	A walnut, 18 in. dia.
32.32	An ash, 24 in. dia.
33.50	Set a post on the south bank of a lake of deep, clear water for corner to fractional sections 21 and 22, from which
	A maple, 16 in. dia., bears S. 33 W., 21 links dist.;
	An ash, 12 in. dia., bears S. 21 E., 34 links dist.
	To obtain the distance across the lake, I send my flagman around the west end thereof, who sets the flag on its north bank, and in the line between sections 21 and 22.
	I now run a base *west* (from the corner on south bank) 5.60 chains, to a point from which the flag bears N. 16° 15' E., and continue said base line west; and at 9 chains and 6 links, a point from which said flag bears N. 25° 15' E., and taking the mean between the results so ascertained, find for the distance across the lake, on the line between sections 21 and 22, 19 chains and 20 links, to which add 33.50 chains, makes
52.70	To the flag on the north bank of the lake.
	Here set a post for corner to fractional sections 21 and 22, from which
	An ash, 16 in. dia., bears N. 21 E., 15 links dist.;
	An elm, 14 in. dia., bears N. 71 W., 23 links dist.
	The point for quarter-section corner, being in the lake, cannot be established.
56.11	An elm, 36 in. dia.
80.00	Set a post for corner to sections 15, 16, 21, 22, from which
	A black oak, 12 in. dia., bears N. 83 E., 23 links dist.;
	A buckeye, 10 in. dia., bears N. 82 W., 17 links dist.;
	A white oak, 14 in dia., bears S. 14 W., 14 links dist.;
	A black oak, 15 in. dia., bears S. 28 E., 24 links dist.
	Land level; rich bottom; not subject to inundation.
	Timber, elm, oak, hickory and ash.

Field-notes of the meanders of Clear Lake.

Begin at the corner to fractional sections 21 and 22, on the north bank, and run thence, in section 22, as follows:
East 10.00 chains; thence
N. 80 E. 12.00 chains; thence
S. 75 E. 5.00 chains; thence
S. 60 E. 5.00 chains; thence
S. 30 E. 5.00 chains; thence
S. 10 W. 6.00 chains; thence
S. 36 W. 8.00 chains; thence
S. 82 W. 10.00 chains; thence
West 10.00 chains; thence
N. 89 W. 8.55 chains, to the corner to fractional sections 21 and 22, on the south bank of the lake; thence, in section 21,
N. 75 W., 9.00 chains, thence
N. 87 W., 10.50 chains, thence
N. 62 W., 8.00 chains, thence ⎫
N. 43 W., 5.50 chains, thence ⎬ At 1.50 chains outlet to lake 20 links wide, runs southwest.
N. 34 W., 4.20 chains, thence ⎭
North, 5.00 chains, thence
N. 35 E., 7.00 chains, thence
N. 55 E., 8.00 chains, thence
East, 5.00 chains, thence
S. 75 E., 3.00 chains, thence
S. 35 E., 6.50 chains, thence

49

Township 25 N., range 2 W., Willamette meridian—Continued.

Chains.	
	S. 67¼ E., 11.10 chains, to the corner to fractional sections 21 and 22, on the north bank of the lake, and place of beginning.
	Land, around this lake, good, rich soil ; banks from 8 to 10 feet high, except at the western part, as far *south* as the outlet, where the land is level and wet.
	Timber, good black oak, hickory, and ash.
	MONDAY, *February* 6, 1854.
	☞ If the deputy should find it more convenient to meander the lake before continuing the line north of it, he will do so.
	East, on a *random* line between sections 15 and 22,
	Variation 17° 46′ east,
40.00	Set a post for temporary quarter-section corner.
58.00	The road from Astoria to Williamsburg bearing N. W. and S. E.
65.50	A stream, 20 links wide, runs south.
79.94	Intersected north and south line 12 links north of the corner to sections 14, 15, 22, and 23, from which corner I run
	West, on a *true* line between sections 15 and 22,
	Variation 17° 41′ east,
39.97	Set a post for quarter-section corner, from which
	A sugar tree, 20 in. dia., bears N. 35 W., 21 links dist.;
	A lynn, 18 in. dia., bears S. 28 E., 81 links dist.
79.94	The corner to sections 15, 16, 21, 22.
	Land, gently rolling , good, rich soil.
	Timber, good ; various kinds of oak, hickory, ash, and sugar tree.
	North, between sections 15 and 16,
	Variation 17° 46′ east,
4.68	An elm, 24 in. dia. .
13.00	Leave timber and enter high rolling prairie, bearing east and west.
16.75	The road from Astoria to Williamsburg bears N. 80 W., and S. 80 E.
40.00	Set a hard flint stone, which cannot be marked, for quarter-section corner ; said stone is 16 in. long, 12 in. wide, and 8 in. thick, and from which a cone white oak, 16 in. dia., bears N. 42 W., 351 links dist.
	No other tree convenient to mark.
50.00	Enter John Orr's field, bearing N. W. and S. E.
55.00	A point 3 chains west of Orr's house ;
61.00	Leave field bearing N. W. and S. E. This field contains about 10 acres ; the line passing through the middle.
80.00	Set a post in mound, with trench, as per instructions, for corner to sections 9, 10, 15, 16, from which corner a granite boulder, four feet in diameter at the surface of the ground, and three feet high, bears N. 72 E., 257 links distant. I cut a cross near the top, facing the corner ; the cross-marks being four inches long, and one-fourth of an inch deep.
	Land high, rolling prairie ; good soil ; not stony, but occasional boulders appear above the natural surface.
	East, on a *random* line between sections 10 and 15,
	Variation 17° 46′ east,
40.00	Set a post for temporary quarter-section corner.
46.50	Leave prairie and enter timber, bearing north, and S. 40 E.
61.40	A stream, 25 links wide, gentle current, muddy bottom, runs south.
79.86	Intersected N. and S. line at the post corner to sections 10, 11, 14, 15, from which corner I run
	West, on a *true* line between sections 10 and 15,
	Variation 17° 46′ east,
39.93	Set a sandstone, 20 in. long, 12 in. wide, and 4 in. thick for quarter-section corner, raise a mound 2 feet high, west side of stone.
	From the stone a bur oak, 16 in. dia., in the eastern edge of the timber, bears N. 75 E., 674 links distant.
79.86	The corner to sections 9, 10, 15, 16.
	Land ; the prairie rolling ; good soil ; timber land level ; 1st rate.
	Timber, oak, hickory, and ash.

Township 25 N., range 2 W., Willamette meridian—Continued.

Chains.	
	North, between sections 9 and 10, Variation 17° 46′ east,
40.00	Set a post for quarter-section corner, raise a mound with trench, as per instructions. A lone bur oak, 10 in. dia., bears S. 75 E., 530 links distant; no other tree near. This corner about 10 chains *west* of a grove of oak and hickory of about 15 acres.
51.25	From this corner Jacob Fry's house, in the north end of grove, bears N. 45 E. A point from which Fry's house bears east, a field of about 10 acres north of the house.
80.00	Deposited a quart of charcoal, and set a post for corner to sections 3, 4, 9, 10, and raised a mound, as per instructions, and planted N. W. 4 white-oak acorns, S. W. wild cherry stones, N. E. beech nuts, and S. E. a butter nut. Land high, rolling prairie; good rich soil, fit for cultivation.
	East, on a *random* line between sections 3 and 10, Variation 17° 46′ east,
40.00	Set a post for temporary quarter-section corner.
55.00	Leave prairie and enter timber, bearing N. and S.
79.90	Intersected N. and S. line 14 links south of the corner to sections 2, 3, 10, 11, from which corner I run West, on a *true* line between sections 3 and 10, Variation 17° 52′ east,
39.95	Set a sand stone, 16 in. long, 12 in. wide, and 4 in. thick, for quarter-section corner, from which a granite boulder, 4 feet long E. and W., by 3½ feet wide N. and S., and 2 feet high above ground, and marked ¼ with a pick, bears N. 31 E., 153 links distant; no other boulder in sight of this corner.
79.90	The corner to sections 3, 4, 9, 10. Land level; good rich soil. Timber, elm, beech, maple, and ash.
	North, on a *random* line between sections 3 and 4, Variation 17° 46′ east,
40.00	Set a post for temporary quarter-section corner.
42.00	Leave prairie and enter timber, bearing S. E. and S. W.
55.15	A spring branch, 10 links wide, runs N. W.
66.50	Enter prairie, bearing N. W. and S. E.
79.95	Intersected the north boundary of the township 30 links east of the corner to sections 3 and 4, from which corner I run South, on a *true* line between sections 3 and 4, Variation 17° 59′ east,
39.95	Set a mulberry post, 6 in. diameter, in the north point of prairie, from which A white oak, 16 in. dia., bears N. 41 E. 195 links; A black oak, 20 in. dia., bears N. 37 W. 205 links.
79.95	The corner to sections 3, 4, 9, 10. Land level, good rich soil, fit for cultivation. Timber, oak, hickory, and elm. *February 7,* 1854.
	All traces of the corner to sections 4, 5, 32 and 33, on the south boundary of the township, having disappeared, I restore and reëstablished said corner in the following manner, viz: Begin at the quarter-section corner the line between sections 4 and 33. One of the witness trees to this corner has fallen down, and the post is gone. The black oak, 18 in. dia., bearing north 25 E. 32 links, standing and sound. I find also the black-oak station tree, 24 in. dia., called for at 37.51 chains; and at 2.49 chains west of the quarter-section corner set a *new* post at the point for quarter-section corner, and mark for witness tree a white oak, 20 in. dia., bears N. 34 W., 37 links dist. West, with the *old* marked line, Variation 18° 25′ east,
40.00	Set a post for temporary corner to sections 4, 5, 32, and 33.

Township 25 N., range 2 W., Willamette meridian—Continued.

Chains.	
80.06	To a point 7 links south of the quarter-section corner on the line between sections 5 and 32. This corner agrees with its description, and from which I run
	East, on the *true* line between sections 5 and 32,
	Variation 18° 22' east,
40.03	Set a lime stone, 18 in. long, 12 in. wide, and 3 in. thick, for reëstablished corner to sections 4, 5, 32 and 33, from which
	A white oak, 12 in. dia., bears N. 21 E., 41 links dist.;
	A white oak, 16 in. dia., bears N. 41 W., 21 links dist.;
	A black oak, 18 in. dia., bears S. 17 W., 32 links dist.;
	A bur oak, 20 in. dia., bears S. 21 E., 37 links dist.
	Thence between sections 4 and 33.
80.06	The quarter-section corner on said line.
	The difference in measurement, being very small, will be rejected.
	North, between sections 32 and 33,
	Variation 17° 40' east,
19.85	A beech, 25 in. dia.
32.37	An elm, 30 in. dia.
40.00	Set a post for quarter-section corner, from which
	A beech, 24 in. dia., bears N. 11 E., 30 links dist.;
	A sugar tree, 20 in. dia., bears S. 40 W., 9 links dist.
48.75	A stream, 20 links wide, rapid current, runs east; general course N. E.
58.20	A sugar tree, 30 in. dia.
75.96	A sugar tree, 25 in. dia.
80.00	Set a post with trench for corner to sections 28, 29, 32, and 33, from which
	An elm, 20 in. dia., bears N. 66 W., 29 links dist.;
	A beech, 10 in. dia., bears S. 16 E., 13 links dist.
	No other trees convenient to mark.
	Planted N. E. 4 hickory nuts, and S. W. 4 cherry stones.
	Land gently rolling; good, rich soil.
	Timber, oak, elm, beech, and sugar tree.
	East, on a *random* line between sections 28 and 33,
	Variation 17ᶜ 40' east,
19.50	A stream 25 links wide, runs north; rapid current. The line crosses about two chains below the mouth of a beautiful spring branch, 10 links wide; comes from the hills on the S. E.
40.00	Set a post for temporary quarter-section corner,
60.00	To foot of hills bearing N. and S.
80.12	Intersected the N. and S. line 7 links north of the corner to 27, 28, 33, and 34, from which corner I run
	West, on a *true* line, between sections 28 and 33,
	Variation 17° 37' east,
40.06	Set a post for quarter-section corner, from which
	A hickory, 10 in. dia., bears N. 25 W., 22 links dist.;
	An elm, 24 in. dia., bears S. 9 W., 14 links dist.
80.12	The corner to sections 28, 29, 32, 33.
	Land, 20 chains, east part very broken; the balance gently rolling; good rich soil.
	Timber, oak, elm, ash, and sugar tree.
	North, between sections 28 and 29,
	Variation 17° 40' east,
17.13	A sugar tree, 30 in. dia.
29.65	A beech, 24 in. dia.
40.00	Set a post for quarter-section corner, from which
	An elm, 14 in. dia., bears N. 6 W., 200 links dist.;
	A white oak, 12 in. dia., bears S. 41 E., 122 links dist.
52.73	A beech, 36 in. dia.
71.15	Top of limestone bluff, 20 feet high, on south bank of Elk Creek, 200 links wide; rapid current, gravelly bottom, runs west; soon turns S. W.
	Enter low wet bottom, on the right bank of creek.

Township 25 N., range 2 W., Willamette meridian—Continued.

Chains.	

80.00	Set a post for corner to sections 20, 21, 28, 29, from which
	    A hickory, 13 in. dia., bears N. 30 E., 16 links dist.;
	    A hickory, 18 in. dia., bears N. 32 W., 22 links dist.;
	    A walnut, 17 in. dia., bears S. 48 W., 40 links dist.;
	    A walnut, 26 in. dia., bears S. 56 E., 34 links dist.
	Land, south of creek, rolling; good, rich soil.
	Timber, oak, elm, beech, and sugar tree; open woods; no undergrowth.

	East, on a *random* line between sections 21 and 28, Variation 17° 40' east,
23.00	A stream, 10 links wide, runs S. W.
40.00	Set a post for temporary quarter-section corner.
43.20	A stream 20 links wide, low, muddy banks and bottoms, runs south.
80.18	Intersected north and south line, 20 links north of the corner to sections 21, 22, 27, 28, from which corner I run West, on a *true* line between sections 21 and 28, Variation 17° 31' east.

40.09	Set a post about 200 links north of the right bank of the creek for quarter-section corner, from which
	    A sugar tree, 14 in. dia., bears N. 57 E., 45 links dist.;
	    A buckeye, 15 in. dia., bears S. 61 W., 61 links dist.

80.18	The corner to sections 20, 21, 28, 29. Land, level; wet bottom; subject to inundation from 4 to 6 feet deep. Timber, oak, hickory, and ash; no undergrowth.
	North, between sections 20 and 21, Variation 17° 40' east,
8.24	A bur oak, 24 in. dia.

28.94	An ash, 15 in. dia., on the S. E. margin of a large lake, across which no sight can be had, because of the water bushes around lake lying principally in section 20, with low, muddy banks; mark said tree for corner to fractional sections 20 and 21, from which
	    A red oak, 15 in. dia., bears S. 35 W., 32 links dist.;
	    A water willow, 10 in. dia., bears S. 21 E. 12 links dist.
	NOTE.—The point for quarter-section corner being in the lake, it cannot be established.
	I now run as follows around the east end of the lake in section 21.
	N. 35 E., 8.00 chains, thence
	N. 10 E., 6.50 chains, thence
	N. 15 W., 5.50 chains, thence
	N. 40 W., 6.70 chains, to a point in the line between sections 20 and 21.
	The northing on the 4 courses of meanders is 23.39 chains, to which add 28.94 chains, makes

52.33	To the point in the line between sections 20 and 21, on the N. E. bank of the lake. Here set a post for corner to fractional sections 20 and 21, from which
	    An elm, 20 in. dia., bears N. 22 E., 24 links dist.;
	    A red oak, 24 in. dia., bears N. 17 W., 21 links dist.

54.20	A stream 25 links wide, gentle current, running S. W. into lake.
57.31	A red oak, 16 in. dia.
72.50	Leave level, rich bottom, and enter upland, bearing E. and W.,

80.00	Set a post for corner to sections 16, 17, 20, 21, from which
	    A black oak, 10 in. dia., bears N. 53 E., 50 links dist.;
	    A beech, 14 in. dia., bears N. 16 W., 14 links dist.;
	    A bur oak, 12 in. dia., bears S. 8 W., 20 links dist.;
	    A beech, 16 in. dia., bears S. 19 E., 15 links dist.
	Land mostly low, level, rich bottom; subject to inundation from 4 to 6 feet deep.
	Timber, oak, beech, maple, and ash; open woods.
	                                        February 8, 1854.

	East, on a *random* line between sections 16 and 21, Variation 17° 40' east,
18.90	A brook, 10 links wide, runs south.

53

Township 25 N., range 2 W., Willamette meridian—Continued.

Chains.	
19.50	Same brook runs north.
21.55	Same brook runs south.
40.00	Set a post for temporary quarter-section corner.
61.50	Enter a small bushy swamp.
70.00	Leave swamp, which contains about 15 acres, and lies mostly in section 21.
80.20	Intersected N. and S. line 16 links north of the corner to sections 15, 16, 21, and 22, from which corner I run West, on a *true* line between sections 16 and 21, Variation 17° 33′ east,
40.10	Set a post for quarter-section corner, from which A beech, 30 in. dia., bears N. 19 W., 31 links dist.; A buckeye, 24 in. dia., bears S. 11 E., 29 links dist.
80.20	The corner to sections 16, 17, 20, 21. Land rolling, 2d rate; wet around swamp. Timber, oak, beech, buckeye, and hickory; thick undergrowth of same and hazel.

	North, between sections 16 and 17, Variation 17° 40′ east,
9.72	A bur oak, 30 in. dia.
26.84	A bur oak, 36 in. dia.
39.00	The road from Astoria to Williamsburg, bearing N. 80 W. and S. 80 E.
40.00	Set a post for quarter-section corner, from which A lynn, 15 in. dia., bears N. 88 W., 17 links dist.; A black oak, 18 in. dia., bears S. 76 E., 21 links dist.
54.20	A white oak, 28 in. dia.
80.00	Set a post for corner to sections 8, 9, 16, 17, from which An elm, 10 in. dia., bears N. 28 E., 5 links dist.; A black oak, 10 in. dia., bears N. 13 W., 48 links dist.; An elm, 12 in. dia., bears S. 41 W., 42 links dist.; A bur oak, 6 in. dia., bears S. 17 E., 105 links dist. Land gently rolling; good, 2d rate. Timber, good quality and open woods, oak, elm, ash, and hickory.

	East, on a *random* line between sections 9 and 16, Variation 17° 40′ east,
40.00	Set a post for temporary quarter-section corner.
45.00	Enter prairie, bearing N. and S.
81.20	Intersected the N. and S. line 22 links north of the corner to sections 9, 10, 15, 16; section 16 is, therefore, out of the proper limits, and I am of opinion that the error is in the measure of the line between sections 9 and 16; re-measure the line *east* of the temporary quarter-section corner, and find it to be 40.18 chains. There was, therefore, an error of one chain in this part of the line, which brings section 16 within its proper limits. From the corner to sections 9, 10, 15, 16, I run West, on a *true* line between sections 9 and 16, Variation 17° 31′ east,
40.10	Set a post for quarter-section corner, from which A white oak, 16 in dia., bears N. 35 E., 32 links dist.; A bur oak, 12 in. dia., bears S. 25 W., 21 links dist.
80.20	The corner to sections 8, 9, 16, 17. Land gently rolling; good, rich soil. The timbered land is open, without undergrowth; oak, hickory, and elm.

	☞ The line between sections 8 and 17 will strike the river in less than 80.00 chains. I therefore run it West, on a *true* line between sections 8 and 17, Variation 17° 40′ east,
8.20	A black oak, 16 in. dia.
27.25	A black walnut, 12 in. dia. Here enter Chickeeles River bottom, bearing north and south.
40.00	Set a post for quarter-section corner, from which

Township 25 N., range 2 W., Willamette meridian—Continued.

Chains.	
	A hickory, 12 in. dia., bears N. 22 E., 10 links dist.;
	An ironwood, 8 in. dia., bears S. 7 E., 2 links dist.
55.10	A hickory, 16 in. dia.
56.50	Set a post on the left bank of Chickeeles River, a navigable stream, for corner to fractional sections 8 and 17, from which
	A hickory, 12 in. dia., bears N. 25 E., 8 links dist.;
	A hackberry, 12 in. dia., bears S. 25 E., 25 links dist.
	Land, the bottom level and rich, upland rolling.
	Timber, oak, hickory, buckeye, &c.
	North, between sections 8 and 9,
	Variation 17° 40' east,
7.42	A walnut, 18 in. dia.
40.00	Set a post for quarter-section corner, from which
	A sugar tree, 9 in. dia., bears N. 35 E., 12 links dist.;
	A walnut, 30 in. dia., bears S. 22 W., 11 links dist.
47.42	A walnut, 18 in. dia.
53.74	A sugar tree, 20 in. dia.
80.00	Set a lime stone, 18 in. long, 12 in. wide, and 4 in. thick, for corner to sections 4, 5, 8, 9, from which
	A sand rock, 4 feet square at the surface of the ground, and 2 feet high, bears N. 47½ E., 341 links dist., marked with a (×) cross, each mark being 6 in. long and ½ in. deep; bearing and distance taken to the cross.;
	A white oak, 36 in. dia., bears N. 24 W., 112 links dist.;
	A white oak, 30 in. dia., bears S. 13 W., 44 links dist.
	No tree in section 9 convenient to mark.
	Land rolling; good, 2d rate.
	Timber, oak, walnut, hickory, and sugar tree.
	Thick undergrowth, same, briers and vines.
	February 9, 1854.
	East, on a *random* line between sections 4 and 9,
	Variation 17° 40' east,
35.60	Leave timber and enter prairie, bearing south and N. E.
40.00	Set a post for temporary quarter-section corner,
43.50	Northwest edge of a small deep pond of about 15 acres, lying mostly in section 9, offset north 400 chains to a point; thence east 9.50 chains to a point; thence south 4 chains to a point on the east bank of the pond, and in the random line between sections 4 and 9,
53.00	*East* of the corner to sections 4, 5, 8, 9,
80.24	Intersected the north and south line 21 links south of the corner to sections 3, 4, 9, 10, from which corner I run
	West, on a *true* line between sections 4 and 9,
	Variation 17° 49' east,
40.12	Set a white oak post, 6 inches diameter, in the eastern edge of prairie for quarter-section corner, from which
	A white oak, 16 in. dia., bears N. 56 W., 497 links dist.;
	A bur oak, 20 in. dia., bears S. 75 W., 512 links dist.
44.75	A black oak, 16 in. dia., in east edge of timber,
80.24	The corner to sections 4, 5, 8, 9.
	Land level; good soil.
	Timber, oak, hickory, and beech; very thick undergrowth; oak and hazel next the prairie.
	The line between sections 5 and 8 will strike Chickeeles River in less than 80 chains, I therefore run it a *true* line
	West, on a *true* line between sections 5 and 8,
	Variation 17° 40' east,
13.77	A white oak, 20 in. dia.
40.00	Set a post for quarter-section corner, from which
	A white oak, 8 in. dia., bears N. 32 W., 4 links dist.;
	A white oak, 10 in. dia., bears S. 45 E., 5 links dist.

Township 25 N., range 2 W., Willamette meridian—Continued.

Chains.	
43.11	A white oak, 40 in. dia.
47.50	Leave broken upland and enter the bottom to Chickeeles River, bearing south and N. E.
60.65	Set a post on the left bank of Chickeeles River, for corner to fractional sections 5 and 8, from which
	A blue ash, 24 in. dia., bears N. 66 E., 4 links dist.;
	An elm, 24 in. dia., bears S. 56 E., 20 links dist.
	Land, upland broken, 3d rate; the bottom level and rich.
	Timber, oak, hickory, &c.; in the bottom, elm and ash; undergrowth, same, pawpaw, spice, and vines.
	The line between sections 4 and 5 will strike Chickeeles River before reaching the *township* line; I therefore run it
	North, on a *true* line between sections 4 and 5,
	Variation 17° 40′ east,
13.75	A cherry, 20 in. dia.;
33.51	A white oak, 24 in. dia.
40.00	Set a post for quarter-section corner, from which
	A white oak, 12 in. dia., bears N. 24 E., 12 links dist.;
	A beech. 28 in. dia., bears S. 44 E., 21 links dist.
	No tree west of the line convenient to mark.
43.15	A white oak, 30 in. dia.
45.50	Leave broken upland and enter Chickeeles River bottom, bearing N. E. and S. W.
56.58	A hackberry, 24 in. dia.
66.50	An elm, 12 in. dia., on the left bank of Chickeeles River; mark it for corner to fractional sections 4 and 5, from which
	A black oak, 14 in. dia., bears S. 10 W., 18 links dist.;
	An elm, 18 in. dia., bears S. 45 E., 35 links dist.
	The upland broken, 3d rate; the bottom level, 1st rate.
	Timber on upland, oak; in bottom, elm, oak, ash, and hickory; undergrowth, pawpaw and spice.
	February 10, 1854.
	The point for corner to sections 5, 6, 31, and 32 being in a deep swamp, and not having been established, I begin at the witness corner on the S. E. edge of the swamp, 4.00 chains east of said point, and run thence east 250 links (with the line between sections 5 and 32) to a point; thence *north* 7.50 chains to a point; thence *west* 6.50 chains to a point on the north edge of the swamp and in the line between sections 31 and 32, and 7.50 chains *north* of the point for corner to sections 31 and 32, on the south boundary of the township. I here set a post for witness point, from which
	A bur oak, 16 in. dia., bears N. 31 E., 25 links dist.;
	An ash, 12 in. dia., bears N. 25 W., 17 links dist.
	From this witness point I run
	North, between sections 31 and 32, counting the distance from the point for corner to said sections in the swamp,
	Variation 17° 40′ east,
12.98	A walnut, 22 in. dia.;
38.19	An ash, 35 in. dia.
40.00	Set a post for quarter-section corner, from which
	A beech, 20 in. dia., bears N. 12 W., 45 links dist.;
	A sugar tree, 20 in. dia., bears S. 12 E., 13 links dist.
57.74	An ash, 24 in. dia.
66.19	A white oak, 36 in. dia.
80.00	Set a post with trench for corner to sections 29, 30, 31, 32, from which
	A beech, 26 in. dia., bears N. 9 W., 12 links dist.;
	A sugar tree, 24 in. dia., bears S. 13 E., 56 links dist.
	And planted N. E. a butter nut, and S. W. 4 cherry stones.
	Land south, half level, north, half rolling; good soil.
	Timber, oak, beech, sugar tree, and walnut; undergrowth, same, and hazel on north part.

Township 25 N., range 2 W., Willamette meridian—Continued.

Chains.	
	East, on a *random* line between sections 29 and 32, Variation 17° 40′ east.
40.00	Set a post for temporary quarter-section corner.
80.16	Intersected the N. and S. line 10 links N. of post corner to sections 28, 29, 32, and 33, from which corner I run West, on a *true* line between sections 29 and 32, Variation 17° 36′ east,
40.08	Set a post for quarter-section corner, from which A black oak, 18 in. dia., bears N. 36 E., 42 links dist.; A bur oak, 20 in. dia., bears S. 43 W., 47 links dist.
80.16	The corner to sections 29, 30, 31, 32. Land gently rolling; good soil; fit for cultivation. Timber, oak, beech, hickory, and walnut; open woods.
	West, on a *true* line between sections 30 and 31, knowing that it will strike the Chickeeles River in less than 80.00 chains. Variation 17° 40′ east,
3.41	A white oak, 15 in. dia.
5.00	Leave upland and enter creek bottom, bearing N. E. and S. W.
8.00	Elk Creek, 200 links wide, gentle current, muddy bottom and banks, runs S. W.
	Ascertain the distance across the creek on the line as follows, viz: Cause the flag to be set on the right bank of the creek, in the line between sections 30 and 31. From the station on the left bank of creek, at 8.00 chains, I run *south* 245 links to a point from which the flag on the right bank bears N. 45 W., which gives for the distance across the creek on the line between sections 30 and 31, 2 chains 45 links.
25.17	A bur oak, 24 in. dia.
40.00	Set a post for quarter-section corner, from which A buckeye, 24 in. dia., bears N. 15 W., 8 links dist.; A white oak, 30 in. dia., bears S. 65 E., 12 links.
41.90	Set a post on the left bank of Chickeeles River, a navigable stream, for corner to fractional sections 30 and 31, from which A buckeye, 16 in. dia., bears N. 50 E., 16 links dist.; A hackberry, 15 in. dia., bears S. 79 E., 14 links dist. Land, low bottom; subject to inundation 3 or 4 feet deep. Timber, buckeye, hackberry, oak, and hickory.
	North, between sections 29 and 30, Variation 17° 40′ east.
6.50	Enter creek bottom, bearing N. E. and S. W.
13.00	Elk creek, 200 links wide, runs S. W.
15.00	Enter a small prairie, about 40 acres.
31.00	Leave prairie and enter timber, bearing E. and W.
40.00	Set a post for quarter-section corner, from which A hickory, 14 in. dia., bears N. 78 E., 16 links dist.; A bur oak, 26 in. dia., bears N. 63 W., 19 links dist.
49.71	A black oak, 30 in. dia.
68.19	A walnut, 36 in. dia.
80.00	Set a post for corner to sections 19, 20, 29, 30, from which A beech, 15 in. dia., bears N. 24 E., 18 links dist.; A blue ash, 24 in. dia., bears N. 79 W., 10 links dist.; A bur oak, 9 in. dia., bears S. 14 W. 10 links dist.; A black oak, 8 in dia., bears S. 11 E., 14 links dist. Land, first half-mile, level prairie, and brushy, oak and hazel; second half-mile, some good timber, oak, &c.; thick undergrowth, same.
	East, on a *random* line between sections 20 and 29, Variation 70° 25′ east,
40.00	Set a post for temporary quarter-section corner.
80.10	Intersected the N. and S. line 20 links north of the corner to sections 20, 21, 28, 29, from which corner I run West, on a *true* line between sections 20 and 29,

Township 25 N., range 2 W., Willamette meridian—Continued.

Chains.	

40.05	Variation 17° 31' east,
	 Set a post for quarter-section corner, from which
	     A sugar tree, 24 in. dia., bears N. 17 W., 20 links dist.;
	     A walnut, 14 in dia., bears S. 10 E., 36 links dist.

80.10	The corner to sections 19, 20, 29, 30. Land level, and rather wet. Timber, oak, sugar tree, beech and walnut; open woods.
	West, on a *random* line between sections 19 and 30, Variation 17° 40' east,
40.00	Set a post for temporary quarter-section corner.
75.53	Intersected the west boundary of the township, 20 links south of the corner to sections 19 and 30, from which corner I run East, on a *true* line between sections 19 and 30, Variation 17° 31' east,

35.52	Set a post for quarter-section corner, from which
	     A sugar tree, 18 in. dia., bears N. 26 W., 23 links dist.;
	     An ash, 10 in. dia., bears S. 86 E., 32 links dist.

75.52	The corner to sections 19, 20, 29, 30. Land level; rich soil; not subject to inundation. Timber, sugar tree, beech, walnut, and ash; undergrowth, spice, prickly ash, and vines. *February* 11, 1854.
	North, between sections 19 and 20, Variation 17° 40' east,
7.70	A bur oak, 20 in. dia.
27.16	A locust, 18 in. dia.
34.00	A pond, 200 links wide, muddy bottom, and low banks; water not so deep as to prevent measuring across on the line with the chain. This pond extends about 15 chains east into section 20, and lies mostly in section 19, extending west.

40.00	Set a post for quarter-section corner, from which
	     A beech, 9 in. dia., bears N. 56 E., 44 links dist.;
	     A lynn, 12 in. dia., bears S. 36 W., 111 links dist.

49.00	The S. W. bank of a lake to be meandered.
	 Set a post for corner to fractional sections 19 and 20, from which
	     A red oak, 12 in dia., bears S. 45 W., 21 links dist.;
	     A lynn, 15 in. dia., bears S. 23 E., 24 links dist.
	 From this corner offset *west* 7.50 chains to a point; thence *north* on an offset line 24.00 chains to a point; thence *east* 7.50 chains to a point in the line between sections 19 and 20, 50 links in advance of lake; thence *south* to N. W. margin of lake, 50 links, where set a post for corner to fractional sections 19 and 20, from which
	     A red oak, 20 in. dia., bears N. 27 E., 31 links dist.;
	     A bur oak, 15 in. dia., bears N. 36 W., 24 links dist.
	 This corner is 72.50 chains *north* of the corner to sections 19, 20, 29, 30, and from which I continue the line between sections 19 and 20 *north*, counting the distance from the corner to sections 19, 20, 29, 30.

80.00	Set a post for corner to sections 17, 18, 19, 20, from which
	     A chestnut, 10 in. dia., bears N. 14 E., 14 links dist.;
	     A buckeye, 12 in. dia., bears N. 86 W., 13 links dist.;
	     A beech, 20 in. dia., bears S. 13 W., 16 links dist.;
	     A buckeye, 20 in. dia., bears S. 27 E., 35 links dist.
	 Land level; rich soil, but too wet for cultivation.
	 Timber, oak, walnut, buckeye, and beech; undergrowth, prickly ash and vines.

	East, on a *random* line between sections 17 and 20, Variation 17° 40' east,
40.00	Set a post for temporary quarter-section corner.
79.90	Intersected N. and S. line 7 links north of post corner to sections 16, 17, 20, 21, from which corner I run

Township 25 N., range 2 W., Willamette meridian—Continued.

Chains.	
	West, on a *true* line between sections 17 and 20,
	Variation 17° 37' east,
39.95	Set a post near the north bank of the lake for quarter-section corner, from which
	A white oak, 12 in. dia., bears N. 33 E., 19 links dist.;
	A white oak, 15 in. dia., bears S. 16 W. 34 links dist.
	From this corner I run south 150 links, to a point on the north bank of the lake, where set a meander corner, from which
	A red oak, 15 in. dia., bears N. 21 E., 15 links dist.;
	An ash, 12 in dia., bears N. 16 W., 12 links dist.
79.90	The corner to sections 17, 18, 19, 20.
	Land level and wet; rich soil.
	Timber, oak, ash, elm, and beech; undergrowth same, briers and vines.

Meanders of Island Lake.

Begin at the corner to fractional sections 19 and 20, on the N. W. margin of the lake, and run thence along the N. W. margin thereof, in fractional section 20, as follows, viz:
N. 79 E., 20.00 chains, thence
N. 84 E., 20.43 chains to the meander corner 150 links *south* of the quarter-section corner, on the line between sections 17 and 20, thence
S. 73 E., 16.00 chains, thence
S. 61 E., 14.00 chains, thence
S. 40¼ E., 19.22 chains, to the corner to fractional sections 20 and 21, on the N. E. bank of lake, at 52.33 chains. At 18.00 chains on this line cross the mouth of a branch, 30 links wide, coming from N. E.
Begin at the corner to fractional sections 20 and 21, on S. E. bank of lake, at 28.94 chains, and run thence along the southern bank of said lake in fractional section 20, as follows:
S. 70 W., 20.00 chains, thence
S. 85 W., 23.00 chains, thence ⎫ *At 14.50 chains cross outlet to lake, 30
N. 70 W., 12.00 chains, thence ⎬ links wide, running W. about 5 chains into
N. 30 W., 18.00 chains, thence* ⎭ pond.
N. 63 W., 20.24 chains, to the corner to fractional sections 19 and 20, at 49.00 chains; thence in section 19 as follows, viz:
N. 75 W., 5.00 chains, thence
N. 60 W., 2.00 chains, thence
N. 10 W., 6.00 chains, thence
N. 10 E., 6.00 chains, thence
N. 25 E., 3.00 chains, thence
N. 38¼ E., 8.48 chains to the corner to fractional sections 19 and 20, on the bank of lake at 72.50 chains.
This lake has low, wet, brushy banks, and has an island of timber in the middle, which ought to be meandered. Timber around lake, ash, maple, and red oak. I cause a flag to be set on the north bank of the island *south* of the meander corner, which is 150 links *south* of the quarter-section corner on the line between sections 17 and 20. From the meander corner run a base 7.50 *east* to a point, from which the flag bears S. 45 W., which gives for the distance across the water to the flag on the island 7.50 chains. Set a meander post in the place of the flag, from which a red oak, 15 in. dia., bears S. 21 W. 24 links, and an ash, 10 in. dia., bears S. 25 E., 17 links dist. From the meander post I run around the island as follows:
S. 62 E., 7.50 chains, thence
S. 55 E., 10.00 chains, thence
S. 20 E., 5.00 chains, thence
South, 4.00 chains, thence
S. 25 W., 6.00 chains, thence
S. 62 W., 5.00 chains, thence
S. 80 W., 4.00 chains, thence
West, 3.50 chains, thence
N. 70 W., 5.00 chains, thence
N. 62 W., 15.00 chains, thence
N. 45 W., 10.00 chains, thence
N. 35 W., 6.00 chains, thence
N. 40 E., 6.50 chains, thence

Township 25 N., range 2 W., Willamette meridian—Continued.

Chains.	
	N. 82 E., 8.00 chains, thence
	S. 88½ E., 14.20 chains, to the meander corner and place of beginning. This island is well timbered, and is good, dry land.
	Timber, oak, hickory, beech, and ash; undergrowth, same and vines.
	The line between sections 18 and 19 will strike the river before reaching the range line; I therefore run it
	West, on a *true* line between sections 18 and 19,
	Variation 17° 40′ east,
7.91	A buckeye, 15 in. dia.;
16.54	A locust, 24 in. dia.
28.90	Set a post on the left bank of Chickeeles River for corner to fractional sections 18 and 19, from which
	A buckeye, 24 in. dia., bears N. 76 E., 22 links dist.;
	A hackberry, 16 in. dia., bears S. 24 W. 15 links.
	There is an island in the river opposite this corner. To ascertain the distance on the line between sections 18 and 19 to the island, I send my flagman across the slough, who sets the flag on the S. E. bank of the island, and in the line between sections 18 and 19, from the corner to said sections on the left bank of the river. I run south 260 links to a point from which the flag on the island bears N. 45¼ W., which gives for the distance 3.79 chains, to which add 28.90 chains, makes
32.69	To the flag. Set a post in the place of the flag for corner to fractional sections 18 and 19, from which
	A white oak, 16 in. dia., bears N. 41 W., 37 links dist.;
	A bur oak, 14 in. dia., bears S. 81 W., 16 links dist.
36.52	A white oak, 20 in. dia.;
39.10	A bur oak, 16 in. dia.
40.00	Set a post for quarter-section corner, from which
	A white oak, 15 in. dia., bears N. 15 W., 21 links dist.;
	A walnut, 20 in. dia., bears S. 21 E., 17 links dist.
45.50	Set a post on the N. W. bank of the island for corner to fractional sections 18 and 19, from which
	A hackberry, 10 in. dia., bears N. 85 E., 15 links dist.;
	A hickory, 15 in. dia., bears S. 51 E., 17 links dist.
	From this corner I meander around the island as follows: In section 19,
	S. 60 W., 10.00 chains, thence
	S. 43 W., 8.00 chains, thence
	South, 2.00 chains, thence
	East, 2.00 chains, thence
	N. 55 E., 4.00 chains, thence
	N. 60 E., 10.00 chains, thence
	N. 66¼ E., 14.15 chains, to the corner to fractional sections 18 and 19, on the S. E. bank of the island, thence in section 18,
	N. 70 E., 10.00 chains, thence
	N. 75 E., 10.00 chains, thence
	N. 25 E., 4.00 chains, thence
	North, 2.50 chains, thence
	West, 1.00 chains, thence
	S. 66 W., 2.00 chains, thence
	S. 75 W., 4.00 chains, thence
	S. 80 W., 10.00 chains, thence
	S. 63½ W., 21.10 chains, to the corner to fractional sections 18 and 19, on the N. W. bank of island, and place of beginning.
	Land, on island and main shore, level and rich; not subject to inundation.
	Timber, oak, hickory, ash, and walnut; undergrowth, same and vines.
	North, between sections 17 and 18,
	Variation 17° 40′ east,
6.57	A hickory, 20 in. dia.
10.80	Set a post on the left bank of Chickeeles River for corner to fractional sections 17 and 18, from which
	A buckeye, 8 in. dia., bears S. 25 W., 15 links dist.;
	A hackberry, 10 in. dia., bears S. 61 E., 3 links dist.

MONDAY, *February* 13, 1854.

Township 25 N., range 2 W., Willamette meridian—Continued.

Meanders of the left bank of Chickeeles River through the township.

Causes.	Distances.	Remarks.
	Chains.	Begin at the corner to fractional sections 4 and 33, in the north boundary of the township and on the left and S. E. bank of the river, and run thence down stream with the meanders of the left bank of said river, in fractional section 4, as follows:
S. 76 W.	18.50	
S. 61 W.	10.00	
S. 59 W.	8.30	To the corner to fractional sections 4 and 5; thence in section 5.
S. 54 W.	10.70	
S. 40 W.	5.60	
S. 50 W.	8.50	
S. 37 W.	17.00	
S. 44 W.	22.00	
S. 38 W.	26.72	To the corner to fractional sections 5 and 8; thence in section 8.
S. 21 W.	16.00	
S. 10 W.	13.00	
South	8.50	To the head of rapids.
S. 9 E.	5.00	
S. 17 E.	20.00	
S. 10 E.	12.00	To foot of rapids.
S. 22¼ E.	8.46	To the corner to fractional sections 8 and 17. Land, along fractional section 8, high, rich bottom; not subject to inundation. The rapids are 37.00 chains long; rocky bottom; estimated fall 10 feet.
		Meanders in section 17.
S. 17 E.	15.00	At 5 chains discovered a vein of coal, which appears to be 5 feet thick, and may be readily worked.
S. 8 E.	12.00	
S. 4 W.	22.00	At 3.00 chains the ferry across the river to Williamsburg, on the opposite side of the river.
S. 25 W.	17.00	
S. 78 W.	12.00	
S. 71 W.	9.55	To the corner to fractional sections 17 and 18; thence in section 18.
S. 65 W.	15.00	
S. 73¾ W.	15.93	To the corner to fractional sections 18 and 19.
S. 65 W.	14.00	In section 19.
S. 60 W.	23.00	
S. 42 W.	10.00	
S. 20 W.	10.00	
S. 16½ W.	13.83	☞ At 2 chains cross outlet to pond and lake, 50 links wide, to the corner to fractional sections 19 and 24, on the range line, 32.50 chains north of the corner to sections 19, 30, 24, and 25.
		Begin at the corner to fractional sections 25 and 30, on the range line 1 chain *south* of the quarter-section corner on said line, and run thence down stream with the meanders of the left bank of Chickeeles River, in fractional section 30, as follows, viz:
S. 41 E.	20.00	At 10 chains discovered a fine mineral spring.
S. 49 E.	15.00	Here appear the remains of an Indian village.
S. 42 E.	12.00	
S. 12¾ E.	5.30	To the corner to fractional sections 30 and 31; thence in section 31.
S. 12 E.	10.00	
S. 12 W.	13.50	To mouth of Elk River, 200 links wide; comes from the east.
S. 41 W.	9.00	At 200 links across the creek.

Township 25 N., range 2 W., Willamette meridian—Continued.

Meanders of the left bank of Chickeeles River through the township.

Causes.	Distances.	Remarks.
	Chains.	
S. 58 W.	11.00	
S. 35 W.	11.00	
S. 20 W.	20.00	At 15 chains mouth of stream, 25 links wide; comes from S. E.,
S. 23¾ W.	8.80	To the corner to fractional sections 31 and 36, on the range line, and 8.56 chains north of the corner to sections 1, 6, 31, and 36, or S. W. corner to this township. Land along the left bank of Chickeeles River is level, rich soil, and only a small part subject to inundation. Timber, oak, hickory, beech, and elm; not much undergrowth. *February* 14, 1854.
Chains.	From the corner to sections 30 and 31, on the west boundary of the township, I run East, on a *true* line between sections 30 and 31, Variation 18° east,
15.10	A white oak, 10 in. dia.
23.50	Intersected the right bank of Chickeeles River, where set a post for corner to fractional sections 30 and 31, from which A black oak, 16 in. dia., bears N. 60 W., 25 links dist.; A white oak, 20 in. dia., bears S. 35 W., 32 links dist. From this corner I run south 12 links, to a point *west* of the corner to fractional sections 30 and 31, on the left bank of the river; thence continue south 314 links, to a point from which the corner to fractional sections 30 and 31, on the left bank of the river, bears N. 72 east; which gives for the distance across the river 9.65 chains. The length of the line between sections 30 and 31 as follows, viz: Part east of river .... 41.90 chains. Part across river .... 9.65 Part west of river .... 23.50 Total .... 75.05 Commence the meanders of section 31 at the corner to fractional sections 31 and 36, on the right bank of Chickeeles River, and run thence up stream with the meanders of the right bank of said river, in fractional section 31, as follows: N. 25 E. 7.00 chains; thence N. 38 E. 11.00 chains; thence N. 50 E. 12.50 chains; thence N. 25 E. 10.00 chains; thence North 13.40 chains, to the corner to fractional sections 30 and 31; thence, in section 30, N. 45 W. 14.00 chains; thence N. 40 W. 12.00 chains; thence N. 34½ W. 10.50 chains, to the corner to fractional sections 25 and 30, on the right bank of Chickeeles River, 27.73 chains north of the corner to sections 25, 30, 31, 36. Land level; rich bottom; not subject to inundation. Timber, oak, hickory, and ash; undergrowth, same, spice and vines.
	From the corner to sections 18, 19, 13, and 24, I run East, on a *true* line between sections 18 and 19, Variation 18° 00′ east,
3.52	A bur oak, 20 in. dia.
17.31	A white oak, 15 in. dia.
21.00	Set a post on the right bank of Chickeeles River for corner to fractional sections 18 and 19, from which

Township 25 N., range 2 W., Willamette meridian—Continued.

Chains.	
	A white oak, 15 in. dia., bears N. 10 E., 31 links dist.; A black oak, 20 in. dia., bears S. 80 W., 15 links dist. From this corner the corner to fractional sections 18 and 19, on the N. W. bank of the island, bears *east*. To obtain the distance across the river between the two corners, I run (from the corner on right bank) *north* 375 links, to a point from which the corner on the island bears S. 68 E.; which gives for the distance 9.27 chains. The length of the line between sections 18 and 19 is 75.77 chains, the several parts of which being as follows: East of river and across the island, including 3.79 chains across the slough .... 45.50 chains. Across the river N. W. of island .... 9.27 West of river .... 21.00 Aggregate, as above 75.77
	From the corner to fractional sections 19 and 24, on the right bank of Chickeeles River, I run up stream with the right bank of said river, in fractional section 19, as follows, viz: N. 30 E. 20.00 chains; thence N. 45¼ E. 15.50 chains, to the corner to fractional sections 18 and 19; thence, in section 18, N. 58 E. 10.00 chains; thence N. 63 E. 17.00 chains; thence N. 75¾ E. 32.12 chains, to a point on the right bank of Chickeeles River *north* of the corner to fractional sections 17 and 18, on the left bank of the river. I here set a post for corner to fractional sections 17 and 18, on the north side of river, from which A black oak, 15 in. dia., bears N. 25 E., 21 links dist.; A black oak, 20 in. dia., bears N. 27 W., 17 links dist. To obtain the distance across the river, on the line between sections 17 and 18, I run a base line *west* 430 links, to a point from which the post corner to fractional sections 17 and 18, on the left and south bank of the river, bears S. 23 east; which gives for the distance 10.13 chains, to which add 10.80 chains, makes
20.93	To the corner to fractional sections 17 and 18, on the right and north bank of the river.

Survey of a claim of 640 acres, confirmed by law to Samuel Williams.

Begin at a black oak, 15 inches diameter, on the right bank of Chickeeles River, opposite the head of a small island in said river. Mark said tree with a blaze, 15 inches long and 6 inches wide, a notch at the top and another at the bottom of the blaze, and on the face of the blaze, with a marking iron, the letters P. S. C., (private survey claim.) From the corner tree
    A black oak, 20 in. dia., bears N. 27 W., 55 links dist.;
    A bur oak, 16 in. dia., bears S. 50 W., 41 links dist.
Both trees marked with a blaze and notch at the lower end of the blaze, facing the corner tree; and on the blaze, with a marking iron, cut the letters W. P. S., (witness private survey.) This is also the S. E. corner of the town of Williamsburg, and from which I run up stream with the meanders of the right bank of Chickeeles River as follows: At an assumed
              Variation 18° 00' east,
North 17.00 chains; at 11.00 chains ferry landing;
N. 12 W. 16.00 chains;
N. 18 W. 20.00 chains; at 14 chains foot of rapids;
N. 12 W. 27.45 chains, to a point on the right bank of the river, where set a post for corner to this survey, from which
    A black oak, 20 in. dia., bears N. 75 W., 33 links dist.;
    A white oak, 20 in. dia., bears S. 43 W., 35 links dist.
NOTE.—At 3 chains on the last course of meanders cross the mouth of stream, 40 links wide; comes from the N. W.
From this corner I run
S. 78 W., with the northern line of this survey,

Township 25 N., range 2 W., Willamette meridian—Continued.

Chains.	
15.17	A black oak, 20 in. dia.
20.00	A stream, 30 links wide, rapid current, runs S. E.
37.51	A bur oak, 20 in. dia.
52.34	A hickory, 16 in. dia.
62.41	A white oak, 20 in. dia.
79.42	Set a post for corner to this survey, from which A black oak, 16 in. dia., bears N. 25 E., 16 links dist.; A white oak, 20 in. dia., bears N. 10 W., 21 links dist.; A white oak, 24 in. dia., bears S. 21 W., 16 links dist.; A black oak, 24 in. dia., bears S. 60 E., 17 links dist.; thence S. 12 E., with the western line of this survey,
10.25	A black oak, 16 in. dia.
17.51	A white oak, 15 in. dia.
41.73	A sugar tree, 20 in. dia.
55.00	The road to Williamsburg, bearing E. and W.
61.53	An elm, 14 in. dia.
80.00	Set a post for corner of this survey, from which A white oak, 16 in. dia., bears N. 73 E., 25 links dist., A white oak, 12 in. dia., bears N. 21 W., 17 links dist.; A black oak, 20 in. dia., bears S. 61 W., 22 links dist.; A black oak, 24 in. dia., bears S. 31 E., 23 links dist.; thence N. 78 E., with the southern line of this survey,
15.73	A black oak, 16 in. dia.
25.31	A black oak, 20 in. dia.
45.61	A white oak, 12 in. dia.
67.20	A white oak, 18 in. dia.
77.68	To the corner tree and place of beginning.
	The land of this claim rolling; good, 2d rate soil, somewhat broken along the rapids in the N. E. part; well timbered, black oak, white oak, hickory, and bur oak; not much undergrowth; some hazel, briers, and vines. The town of Williamsburg, situated on the S. E. part of the claim, is pleasantly located on the right bank of the river, some 8 or 10 feet above high water, and has at this time sixteen families residing in it. Some three or four tenements are now being constructed within the limits of the town. *February* 15, 1851.

	From the corner to fractional sections 17 and 18, on the right and north bank of Chickeeles River, 20.93 chains north of the corner to sections 17, 18, 19, 20, I run North, between sections 17 and 18, counting the distance from the corner to sections 17, 18, 19, 20, Variation 18° east,
22.73	A black oak, 20 in. dia.
36.45	Intersected the southern line of Samuel Williams's claim, where set a post for corner to fractional sections 17 and 18, from which A black oak, 16 in. dia., bears S. 50 W., 22 links dist.; A white oak, 20 in. dia., bears S. 21 E., 31 links dist. From this corner I run N. 78 E., along the southern line of the said claim, 20.15 chains, to the corner tree on the right bank of Chickeeles River and S. E. corner of said claim; thence down stream, on the right bank of said river, in fractional section 17, as follows: S. 16 W. 10.00 chains; thence S. 45 W. 10.00 chains; thence S. 72 W. 10.30 chains, to the corner to fractional sections 17 and 18.

Field-notes of the survey of a small island in Chickeeles River, lying wholly in section 17.

Cause the flag to be set on the head of the island, at a point bearing S. 45 E. from the black oak tree, the S. E. corner to Samuel Williams's claim; from said corner tree run S. 45 W. 215 links, to a point *west* of the flag on the head of the island; which gives for the distance from the corner tree to the flag 215 links. Set a meander post in the place of the flag, from which
A bur oak, 16 in. dia., bears S. 10 W., 15 links dist.;

Township 25 N., range 2 W., Willamette meridian—Continued.

Chains.	
	A white oak, 12 in. dia., bears S. 15 E., 21 links dist. From the meander post I run around the island as follows: S. 16 W. 9.00 chains; thence S. 45 W. 10.00 chains; thence S. 10 W. 2.00 chains; thence South 1.50 chains, to the lower end of island; thence East 1.50 chains; thence N. 75 E. 4.00 chains; thence N. 50 E. 5.00 chains; thence N. 30 E. 6.00 chains; thence N. 10 E. 6.00 chains; thence N. 10 W. 3.00 chains; thence N. 73 W. 29β chains, to the meander post and place of beginning. This island is well timbered; white and black oak and hickory; not subject to inundation; undergrowth, same, spice, and vines.
	From the corner to sections 7, 18, 12, and 13, on the range line, I run East, on a *true* line between sections 7 and 18, Variation 18° 00' east,
7.93	Intersected the western line of Samuel Williams's survey of 640 acres, and at said intersection set a post for corner to fractional sections 7 and 18, from which A white oak, 15 in. dia., bears N. 25 W., 15 links dist.; A black oak, 20 in. dia., bears S. 34 W., 19 links dist. From this corner I run N. 12 W., with the western line of said Williams's claim, 23.23 chains, to the N. W. corner thereof. Land gently rolling. Timber, oak and hickory.
	From the corner to fractional sections 17 and 18, in the southern line of Samuel Williams's survey, and 36.45 chains *north* of the corner to sections 17, 18, 19, 20, I run North, on a *blank* line passing through Samuel Williams's survey, counting the distance from the corner to said sections 17, 18, 19, 20, Variation 18° 00' east,
40.00	Point for quarter-section corner *in* Samuel Williams's survey; corner not established.
52.50	The road leading into Williamsburg.
80.00	Set a temporary corner to sections 7, 8, 17, 18, in said Williams's claim. This line passes through the back part of the town of Williamsburg, but I make no connection with the lines of said town.
	North, on a *blank* line between sections 7 and 8, Variation 18° 00' east,
12.50	To creek, 30 links wide; runs east; comes from N. W.
38.10	Intersected the north boundary of Samuel Williams's survey, where set a post for corner to fractional sections 7 and 8, from which A black oak, 10 in. dia., bears N. 10 E., 15 links dist.; A bur oak, 15 in. dia., bears N. 16 W., 17 links dist. From this corner I run N. 78 E., on the north line of said claim, 440 links, to the N. E. corner thereof, on the right bank of Chickeeles River. From the corner of fractional sections 7 and 8, in the north line of Samuel Williams's survey, North, on a *true* line between sections 7 and 8, counting the distance from the temporary corner to sections 7, 8, 17, 18, within said Williams's survey,
40.00	Set a post for quarter-section corner, from which A black oak, 15 in. dia., bears N. 25 E., 16 links dist.; A white oak, 16 in. dia., bears N. 73 W., 12 links dist.
45.17	A white oak, 18 in. dia.
63.71	A bur oak, 15 in. dia.
80.00	Set a post for corner to sections 5, 6, 7, 8, from which

Township 25 N., range 2 W., Willamette meridian—Continued.

Chains.	
	A red oak, 20 in. dia., bears N. 20 E., 40 links dist.;
	A white oak, 16 in. dia., bears N. 16 W., 43 links dist.;
	A red oak, 24 in. dia., bears S. 80 W., 39 links dist.;
	A white oak, 40 in. dia., bears S. 75 E., 22 links dist.
	Land gently rolling; good rich soil.
	Timber, oak, hickory, and ash.
	February 16, 1854.

	East, on a *true* line between sections 5 and 8, Variation 18° 00′ east,
5.16	A white oak, 15 in. dia.
7.41	A bur oak, 12 in. dia.
10.50	Set a post on the right bank of Chickeeles River for corner to fractional sections 5 and 8, west of river, from which
	A red oak, 30 in. dia., bears N. 58 W., 5 links dist.;
	A hickory, 12 in. dia., bears S. 42 W., 5 links dist.
	From this corner the post corner to fractional sections 5 and 8, on the left bank of the river, bears S. 89 E.
	From a point 16 links *south* of this corner, and *west* of the corner to fractional sections 5 and 8, on the left and east bank of the river, I run north 454 links, to a point from which the corner post on the left bank of the river bears S. 63 E., which gives for the distance across the river 8.91 chains. The length of the line between sections 5 and 8, including the distance across the river, is, therefore, 80.06 chains, viz:
	East of river .... 60.65 chains.
	Across river 8.91
	West of river 10.50
	Total 80.06

	West, on a *random* line between sections 6 and 7, Variation 18° 00′ east,
25.10	A stream, 25 links wide, gentle current, runs south.
40.00	Set a post for temporary quarter-section corner.
56.00	A stream, 15 links wide, runs S. E.
76.26	Intersected the west boundary 21 links north of the corner to sections 6 and 7, from which corner I run
	East, on a *true* line between sections 6 and 7, Variation 18° 09′ east,
36.26	Set a post for quarter-section corner, from which
	A black oak, 16 in. dia., bears N. 15 W., 21 links dist.;
	A white oak, 40 in. dia., bears S. 21 W., 33 links dist.
76.26	The corner to sections 5, 6, 7, 8.
	Land hilly; 2d rate.
	Timber, oak, sugar tree, and hickory; undergrowth, same and hazel.

	North, on a *random* line between section 5 and 6, Variation 18° 00′ east,
20.00	Enter windfall, bearing N. 60 W. and S. 60 E.
35.00	Leave windfall, having same bearings.
40.00	Set a post for temporary quarter-section corner.
80.06	Intersected the north boundary of the township 24 links east of the corner to sections 5 and 6, from which corner I run
	South, on a *true* line between said sections 5 and 6, Variation 18° 10′ east,
40.06	Set a post for quarter-section corner, from which
	A hickory, 20 in. dia., bears N. 18 E., 27 links dist.;
	A white oak, 24 in. dia., bears S. 31 W., 18 links dist.
80.06	The corner to sections 5, 6, 7, 8.
	Land rolling, and 2d rate.
	Timber, oak, hickory, sugar tree, and ash; undergrowth, same and hazel.

Township 25 N., range 2 W., Willamette meridian—Continued.

Chains.	
	From the corner to sections 4, 5, 32, and 33, on the north boundary of the township, I run South, on a *true* line between sections 4 and 5, Variation 18° 00' east,
2.10	A white oak, 15 in. dia.
4.00	Set a post on the right bank of Chickeeles River for corner to fractional sections 4 and 5, from which A bur oak, 16 in dia., bears N. 25 E., 34 links dist.; A black oak, 20 in. dia., bears N. 33 W., 21 links dist. From this corner the post corner to fractional sections 4 and 5, on the left bank of the river, bears S. ¼ W. To obtain the distance across the river I run (from the corner on the right bank) N. 89° 30' W. 326 links, to a point from which the post corner to fractional sections 4 and 5, on the left bank, bears S. 18° 30' E., which gives for the distance 9.46 chains. The length of the line between sections 4 and 5 will, therefore, be as follows, viz:
	Part south of the river .... 66.50 chains.
	Part across the river 9.46
	Part north of the river 4.00
	Aggregate 79.96

From the corner to fractional sections 4 and 33, on the right bank of Chickeeles River, I run down stream with the meanders of the right and N. W. bank of said river as follows, viz:
In section 4—
S. 40° 45' W. 5.35 chains, to the corner to fractional sections 4 and 5; thence, in section 5,
S. 72 W. 11.00 chains; thence
S. 55 W. 20.00 chains; thence
S. 40 W. 20.00 chains, (at this point the bluff comes to the river;) thence
S. 42 W. 18.00 chains; thence
S. 40 W. 18.00 chains; thence
S. 18¼ W. 19.75 chains, to the corner to fractional sections 5 and 8.
Land rolling along the last three courses, which are under a bluff bank from 20 to 30 feet high; the bottom, along the first three courses of meanders, good, rich land.
Timber, oak, hickory, ash, elm, and buckeye; undergrowth, same and vines in the bottom.

From the corner to fractional sections 5 and 8, on the right bank of the river, I continue the meanders down stream, along fractional section 8, as follows, under a bluff bank from 20 to 30 feet high:
S. 26 W. 9.70 chains; thence
S. 10 W. 15.00 chains; thence
South 15.00 chains, to the head of rapids; thence
S. 12 E. 2.55 chains, to the corner to fractional section 8 and N. E. corner of Samuel Williams's claim. Mark the black oak witness tree to this corner, bearing N. 75 W., 33 links distant, "Section 8."
Land rolling, and rather broken along the river.
Timber, principally oak.

February 17, 1854.

Private claim surveyed after public survey.

Survey of a claim of 640 acres, confirmed by law to Daniel Reed.
Begin at the corner to fractional sections 5 and 8, on the left bank of Chickeeles River.
The corner post standing, and witness trees agree with the description furnished me, viz:
A blue ash, 24 in. dia., bears N. 66 E., 4 links dist.;
An elm, 24 in. dia., bears S. 56 E., 20 links dist.
From this corner I run down stream with the meanders of the left and east bank of said river S. 21 W. 16.00 chains, to a point where set a post on the

Township 25 N., range 2 W., Willamette meridian—Continued.

Chains.	
	left and east bank of Chickeeles River for the S. W. corner of the said Reed's claim, from which
	A black oak, 16 in. dia., bears N. 44 E., 37 links dist.
	This tree marked with a blaze, 15 inches long, 6 inches wide, facing the corner post, with two notches—one at the upper end and the other at the lower end of the blaze; also marked with a marking iron on the face of the blaze the letters D. R., (Daniel Reed,) W. P. C., (witness private claim.)
	A bur oak, 20 in. dia., bears S. 47 E., 45 links dist.
	Marked with a blaze and notch at the lower end of the blaze facing the corner post, with the letters R. 2 W., T. 25 N., sec. 8.
	From the corner post I run
	S. 54 E. along the S. W. boundary line of said claim,
	Variation 17° 40′ east,
10.51	A bur oak, 16 in. dia.
20.67	A black oak, 20 in. dia.
31.00	Leave river bottom and enter upland, bearing N. and S.
44.73	A white oak, 24 in. dia.
57.34	A white oak, 20 in. dia.
77.90	Set a post for corner of this claim and fractional section 8, from which
	A white oak, 16 in. dia., bears N. 40 W., 31 links dist.
	This tree marked with a blaze and two notches facing the corner post—one notch above and the other below the blaze. Mark the letters W. P. C. (witness private claim) on the face of the blaze.
	A black oak, 20 in. dia., bears S. 10 W., 21 links dist.;
	A bur oak, 15 in. dia., bears S. 45 E., 13 links dist.
	Both trees marked with a blaze and notch facing the post, and S. 8 with a marking iron.
	From this corner I run
	N. 36 E. along the southeastern line of this claim,
	Variation 17° 40′ east,
3.41	A white oak, 15 in. dia.
5.45	Intersected the line between sections 8 and 9, where set a post for corner to fractional sections 8 and 9, from which
	A white oak, 16 in. dia., bears S. 25 W., 22 links dist.;
	A bur oak, 20 in. dia., bears S. 37 E., 18 links dist.
	From this corner I run *south* with the line between said sections 23.70 chains, to the corner to sections 8, 9, 16, 17.
33.73	A white oak, 15 in. dia.
41.17	A bur oak, 16 in. dia.
57.31	A white oak, 20 in. dia.
60.57	A black oak, 30 in. dia.
64.00	Leave timber and enter prairie, bearing N. and S.
75.17	Intersected the line between sections 4 and 9, where set a post with mound and trench for corner to fractional sections 4 and 9.
	Plant N. E. a hickory nut, S. E. 4 apple seeds.
	To obtain the distance on the line between sections 4 and 9, from the fractional-section corner just established to the corner to sections 3, 4, 9, 10, I run as follows:
	North 4.00 chains (to avoid the pond) to a point; thence *east* on an offset line 12.00 chains to a point; thence *south* 4.00 chains, to the line between said sections 4 and 9; thence *east* with said line, and at 39.33 chains, the corner to sections 3, 4, 9, 10, the distance being counted from the corner to fractional sections 4 and 9, in the S. E. line of Daniel Reed's claim.
80.00	To a point for the east corner of the claim. Set a lime stone, 10 inches square and 6 inches thick, and post with mound and trench, as per instructions, for corner to said claim and to fractional section 4. From the corner a white oak, 16 in. dia., standing in the edge of the timber, bears N. 65 W., 555 links distant. Mark said tree with a blaze and two notches—one above and the other below the blaze—facing the corner. With a marking iron cut the letters W. P. C. (witness private claim) on the face of the blaze. This corner about 3.00 chains N. W. of a small pond. Thence I run
	N. 54 W. along the N. E. boundary line of this claim,
	Variation 17° 40′ east,
5.50	Leave prairie and enter timber, bearing N. E. and S. W.
10.53	A bur oak, 15 in. dia.
25.34	A black oak, 16 in. dia.
54.07	Intersected the line between sections 4 and 5.

Township 25 N., range 2 W., Willamette meridian—Continued.

Chains.	
	Here set a post for corner to fractional sections 4 and 5, from which
	A black oak, 16 in. dia., bears N. 43 E., 22 links dist.;
	A white oak, 20 in. dia., bears N. 37 W., 17 links dist.
	From this corner I run *north* with the line between said sections 4 and 5, and at 30.81 chains, the corner to fractional sections 4 and 5, on the left and south bank of Chickeeles River.
64.00	Leave upland, and enter river bottom, bearing N. E. and S. W.
65.50	A bur oak, 20 in. dia.
71.53	A bur oak, 16 in. dia.
75.36	A walnut, 36 in. dia.
77.90	Set a post on the left and S. E. bank of Chickeeles River, for corner of this claim and fractional section 5, from which
	A white oak, 16 in. dia., bears N. 60 E., 31 links dist.
	Marked with a blaze and notch facing the post, and section 5 on the face of the blaze.
	A bur oak, 15 in. dia., bears S. 40 E., 37 links dist.
	Marked with a blaze and two notches facing the post. The letters W. P. C. (witness private claim) cut with a marking iron on the face of the blaze.
	From this corner I run up stream with the meanders of the left and S. E. bank of the river in fractional section 5.
	N. 37 E., 1.00 chains, thence
	N. 50 E., 8.50 chains, thence
	N. 40 E., 5.60 chains, thence
	N. 54 E., 10.70 chains, to the corner to fractional sections 4 and 5, on the left bank of the river.
	From the corner to fractional section 5, and the upper corner to the claim on the left bank of Chickeeles River, I run down stream with the meanders of the left bank of said river, within the claim, as follows:
	S. 37 W., 16.00 chains, thence
	S. 44 W., 22.00 chains, thence
	S. 38 W., 26.72 chains, to the original corner to fractional sections 5 and 8, on the left and east bank of Chickeeles River, and place of beginning.
	Land, much the largest portion of this claim gently rolling upland; good, 2d rate timber, oak, walnut, hickory, and sugar tree. The bottom land along the river is dry, rich land, not subject to inundation.
	Timber, walnut, oak, hickory, and hackberry; undergrowth same, briers and vines.
	February 18, 1854.

GENERAL DESCRIPTION.

The quality of the land in this township is considerably above the common average. There is a very fair proportion of rich bottom land, chiefly situated on both sides of Chickeeles River, which is navigable through the township for steamboats of light draught, except over the rapids in section 8. These rapids are 37 chains long; estimated fall, about 10 feet.

The uplands are generally rolling, good 1st and 2d rate land, and well adapted for cultivation. Elk River is a beautiful stream of clear water, running through the southern part of the township, and emptying into Chickeeles River, in section 31. There is a fine mill-seat on this stream in section 22.

Timber, chiefly oak, beech, hickory, hackberry, and sugar tree, and is very equally distributed over the township, except in the prairie embracing parts of sections 3, 4, 9, 10, 15, and 16.

The town of Williamsburg was laid out by Samuel Williams, some two years since, on the right bank of Chickeeles River, a little below the foot of the rapids. It now contains sixteen houses, and others are being built; has a good landing in front, with a ferry, and has the appearance of thrift and prosperity.

There are several good quarries of stone (principally lime) along the Chickeeles and Elk Rivers, which will afford inexhaustible quantities of excellent building materials. On the line between sections 1 and 12 I discovered gold dust and auriferous quartz, and in section 17, on the left bank of Chickeeles River, opposite Williamsburg, a valuable coal bank. There are three settlements—one on the N. W. quarter of section 10, one on the N. W. quarter of section 15 and N. E. quarter of section 16, and the other on the N. E. quarter of section 23 and N. W. quarter of section 24.

A valuable salt spring was discovered crossing the south boundary of section 31, running N. W.; also the remains of an Indian village on the left bank of Chickeeles River, in section 30. Fossil remains on the west bank of a small lake in section 26, and ancient works on the left bank of Elk River, in the N. E. quarter of section 27.

LIST OF NAMES.

A list of the names of the individuals employed to assist in running, measuring, or marking the lines and corners described in the foregoing field notes of township No. 25, north of the base line of range No. 2, west of the Willamette meridian, showing the respective capacities in which they acted: Peter Long, chainman; John Short, chainman; George Sharp, axeman; Adam Dull, axeman; Henry Flagg, compassman.

We hereby certify that we assisted Robert Acres, deputy surveyor, in surveying the exterior boundaries and subdividing township number twenty-five north of the base line of range number two west of the Willamette meridian, and that said township has been in all respects, to the best of our knowledge and belief, well and faithfully surveyed, and the boundary monuments planted according to the instructions furnished by the surveyor general.

PETER LONG, *Chainman.*
JOHN SHORT, *Chainman.*
GEORGE SHARP, *Axeman.*
ADAM DULL, *Axeman.*
HENRY FLAGG, *Compassman.*

Subscribed and sworn to by the above named persons, before me, a justice of the peace for the county of ———, in the State (or Territory) of ———, this —— day of ———, 185 .

HENRY DOOLITTLE,
Justice of the Peace.

I, Robert Acres, deputy surveyor, do solemnly swear that, in pursuance of a contract with ——— ———, surveyor of the public lands of the United States in the State (or Territory) of ———, bearing date the —— day of ———, 185 , and in strict conformity to the laws of the United States and the instructions furnished by the said surveyor general, I have faithfully surveyed the exterior boundaries (or subdivision and meanders, as the case may be) of township number twenty-five north of the base line of range number two west of the Willamette meridian, in the ——— aforesaid, and do further solemnly swear that the foregoing are the true and original field notes of such survey.

ROBERT ACRES,
Deputy Surveyor.

Subscribed by said Robert Acres, deputy surveyor, and sworn to before me, a justice of the peace for ——— County, in the State (or Territory) of ———, this —— day of ———, 185

HENRY DOOLITTLE,
Justice of the Peace.

To each of the original field books, the surveyor general will append his official approval, according to the following form, or so varied as to suit the facts in the case:

SURVEYOR'S OFFICE AT ——— ———,
——— ———, 185 .

The foregoing field notes of the survey of (here describe the survey) executed by Robert Acres, under his contract of the —— day of ———, 185 , in the month of ———, 185 , having been critically examined, the necessary corrections and explanations made, the said field notes, and the surveys they describe, are hereby approved.

A. B.,
Surveyor General.

To the copies of the field notes transmitted to the seat of Government, the surveyor general will append to each township the following certificate:

I certify that the foregoing transcript of the field notes of the survey of the (here describe the character of the surveys, whether meridian, base line, standard parallel, exterior township lines, or subdivision lines, and meanders of a particular township) in the State (or Territory) of ———, has been correctly copied from the original notes on file in this office.

A. B.,
Surveyor General.

Table showing the difference of latitude and departure in running 80 chains at any course from 1 to 60 minutes.

Minutes.	Links.	Minutes.	Links.	Minutes.	Links.
1	$2\frac{1}{3}$	21	49	41	$95\frac{2}{3}$
2	$4\frac{2}{3}$	22	$51\frac{1}{3}$	42	98
3	7	23	$53\frac{2}{3}$	43	$100\frac{1}{3}$
4	$9\frac{1}{3}$	24	56	44	$102\frac{2}{3}$
5	$11\frac{2}{3}$	25	$58\frac{1}{3}$	45	105
6	14	26	$60\frac{2}{3}$	46	$107\frac{1}{3}$
7	$16\frac{1}{3}$	27	63	47	$109\frac{2}{3}$
8	$18\frac{2}{3}$	28	$65\frac{1}{3}$	48	112
9	21	29	$67\frac{2}{3}$	49	$114\frac{1}{3}$
10	$23\frac{1}{3}$	30	70	50	$116\frac{2}{3}$
11	$25\frac{2}{3}$	31	$72\frac{1}{3}$	51	119
12	28	32	$74\frac{2}{3}$	52	$121\frac{1}{3}$
13	$30\frac{1}{3}$	33	77	53	$123\frac{2}{3}$
14	$32\frac{2}{3}$	34	$79\frac{1}{3}$	54	126
15	35	35	$81\frac{2}{3}$	55	$128\frac{1}{3}$
16	$37\frac{1}{3}$	36	84	56	$130\frac{2}{3}$
17	$39\frac{2}{3}$	37	$86\frac{1}{3}$	57	133
18	42	38	$88\frac{2}{3}$	58	$135\frac{1}{3}$
19	$44\frac{1}{3}$	39	91	59	$137\frac{2}{3}$
20	$46\frac{2}{3}$	40		60	140

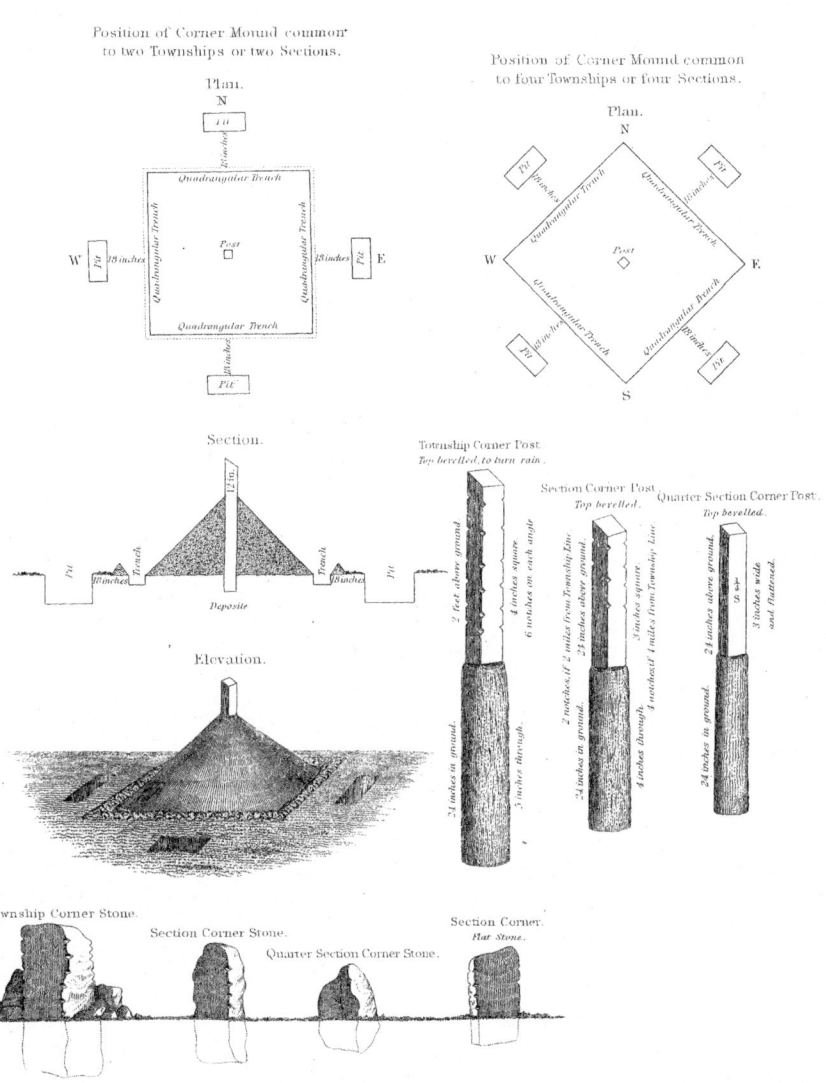

C.

Diagram for the

illustration of Mound, Stake, and Stone corner boundaries.

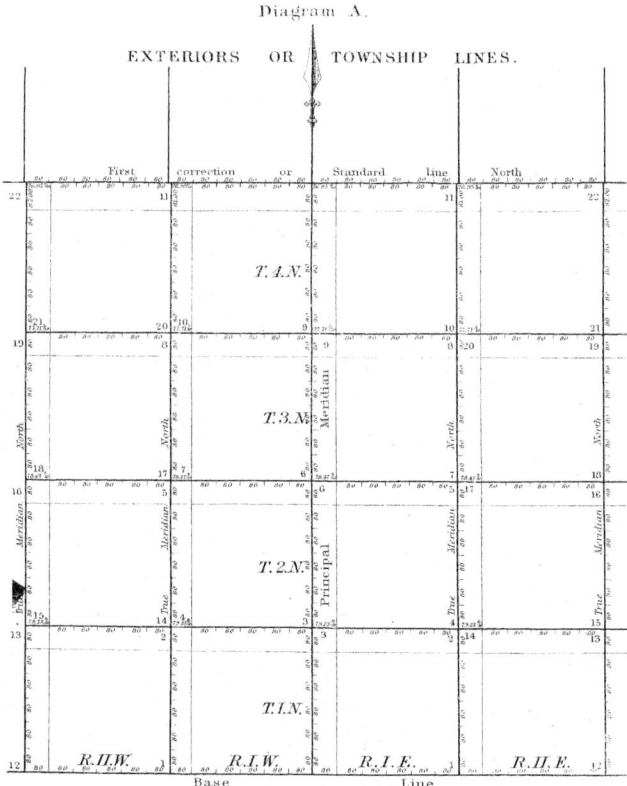

A TREATISE

ON THE

MAGNETIC DECLINATION

OR

VARIATION OF THE NEEDLE.

[DESIGNED TO TAKE THE PLACE OF THE CHAPTER COMMENCING AT THE FOOT OF PAGE 25 AND ENDING IN THE MIDDLE OF PAGE 29 OF THE MANUAL OF INSTRUCTIONS TO SURVEYORS-GENERAL OF THE UNITED STATES, PRINTED IN 1871, A PART OF WHICH HAS BECOME OBSOLETE.]

WASHINGTON:
GOVERNMENT PRINTING OFFICE.
1878.

DEPARTMENT OF THE INTERIOR, GENERAL LAND OFFICE,
Washington, D. C., February 21, 1878.

The following tables were prepared by direction of Hon. Carlile P. Patterson, Superintendent of the United States Coast Survey, in accordance with a request of the Commissioner of the General Land Office.

At the suggestion of J. E. Hilgard, esq., assistant in charge of the Coast Survey Office, a chapter has been added entitled "The Magnetic Declination, or Variation of the Needle."

The treatise is designed to take the place of the chapter commencing at the foot of page 25 and ending in the middle of page 29 of the "Manual of Instructions to surveyors-general of the United States," printed in 1871, a part of which in the course of time has become obsolete. It will be found of great interest and value as an aid in the promotion of improvement in the manner of prosecuting surveys of public lands.

STEPHEN J. DALLAS,
Principal Clerk of Surveys.

THE MAGNETIC DECLINATION OR VARIATION OF THE NEEDLE.

The magnetic declination at any place is the angle which the compass needle, when it is correctly constructed and freely suspended, makes with the true meridian. The true meridian is fixed, but the declination varies because the direction in which the needle points is in a continuous state of change. Therefore, whenever a measure of the declination of the needle is taken, the exact time (year, day of month, and hour of the observations) should be recorded as well as the geographical position of the place, or its latitude and longitude expressed to the nearest minutes of arc.

The declination is called "West" when the north end of the needle points to the west of the true meridian, and it is called "East" when the north end of the needle points east of the true meridian. In order to give an idea of the amount of the declination at present observable within the limits of the United States we instance the following places at or near which it reaches extreme value, which are given to the nearest whole degree.

At Eastport, Me, the declination is 18° west.
At the mouth of the Rio Grande, Texas, 8° east.
At San Diego, Cal., 14° east.
At Sitka, Alaska, 29° east.
At Fort Yukon, Alaska, 36° east.

The accuracy with which the declination may be determined depends chiefly upon the instrumental means, but also, and in a great measure, upon the care taken in the use of the instruments and the selection of the proper methods and times for observing.

The instruments ordinarily at the disposal of the surveyor are sufficiently described, but for a description and illustration of more refined ones, as used by scientists, we refer to the instructions for magnetical observations published as Appendix No. 16, Coast Survey Report for 1875.

Omitting any detailed notice of the irregular variations to which the magnetic needle is subject, it becomes important for the purposes of the surveyor to refer particularly to the changes which have a special bearing upon his observations. These are the *daily variation* and the *secular variation*.

The daily variation.—It has been found that at about the time of sunrise the north end of the needle has a slow motion towards the east which soon ceases. The needle is then said to be at its eastern elongation; its north end then begins a retrograde motion towards the west, and at about one o'clock in the afternoon reaches the point at which it is said to be at its western elongation, after which it again turns back towards the east.

The times at which the needle reaches its eastern and western elongations vary with the seasons of the year (with the sun's declination), happening a little earlier in summer than in winter.

The angular range between the eastern and western elongations varies also with the season of the year.

The average position of the needle for the day is called the *mean magnetic meridian.*

At about six o'clock in the evening (and for about an hour before and after), throughout the year, the position of the needle coincides very nearly with the mean magnetic meridian, and this, therefore, is the time most favorable for making observations to obtain at once the mean declination.

For reducing the direction of the needle observed at other hours to the mean magnetic meridian the following table is furnished. It gives to the nearest minute the variations of the needle from its average position during the day, for each hour in the day for the four seasons of the year.

Table for reducing the observed declination to the mean declination of the day.

	The needle points east of the mean magnetic meridian.					The needle points west of the mean magnetic meridian.						
	A. M.	A. M.	A. M.	A. M.	A. M.	A. M.	Noon.	P. M.	P. M.	P. M.	P. M.	P. M.
Hour	h. 6	h. 7	h. 8	h. 9	h. 10	h. 11	Noon.	h. 1	h. 2	h. 3	h. 4	h. 5	h. 6
Spring	3'	4'	4'	3'	1'	1'	4'	5'	4'	3'	2'	1'
Summer	4	5	5	4	1	2	4	6	5	4	3	2	1
Autumn	2	3	3	2	0	2	3	4	3	2	1	1	0
Winter	1	1	2	2	1	0	2	3	3	2	1	1	0

The secular variation of the magnetic declination is a subject of the greatest importance to surveyors. It manifests itself by a gradual change in one direction, which at first increases slowly, then more rapidly, diminishing again afterward until the needle becomes stationary and subsequently returns by similar changes to its former position, the whole period extending over nearly two and a half centuries. Thus it will be seen by a table given below that at Philadelphia the declination was $8\frac{3}{4}°$ west in 1700, whence it diminished until in 1800 it reached a minimum 2°.1 (2° 6'), and will increase again to 6°.8 in 1880. At present all along the Atlantic and Gulf coasts the effect of the secular variation is to *increase* west declinations or to *decrease* east declinations by from 2' to 5', but on the Pacific coast the effect is opposite in direction, viz, *increasing* east declinations by from 1' to 3'.

In Alaska, however, we have indications of a decrease of east declinations.

The following table of computed declinations at various places, taken from the Coast Survey Report for 1874, exhibits the effect of the secular variation for a number of places, and will be found especially useful where old lines have to be retraced.

The table should not be extended in time either way without the support of additional observations.

TABLE OF DECIMAL VALUES OF THE MAGNETIC DECLINATION.

[From the Coast Survey Report of 1874, Appendix No. 8, with improvements].

This table has been constructed to facilitate the reduction of observed declinations from one epoch to another; it will be found specially useful when old lines run by compass have to be retraced, and for the construction of isogonic charts for a given epoch. A + sign indicates west; a − sign east declination.

Year (Jan. 1).	Halifax, Nova Scotia.	Quebec, Canada.	York Factory, Hudson Bay.	Portland, Me.	Burlington, Vt.	Rutland, Vt.	Portsmouth, N. H.	Newburyport, Mass.	Salem, Mass.	Boston, Mass.	Cambridge, Mass.	Nantucket, Mass.	Providence, R. I.	Hartford, Conn.	New Haven, Conn.	Albany, N. Y.	Oxford, N. Y.	Buffalo, N. Y.	Erie, Pa.	Cleveland, Ohio.	Detroit, Mich.
1640		15.9	+18.6																		
50		16.4	19.2																		
60		16.5	18.8																		
70		16.4	17.2																		
80		15.9	14.8																		
90		15.2	11.6				+10.4			+10.0	9.8										
1700			+4.0				9.5			9.3	9.2										
10	+12.5	+11.2	−0.1				8.9			8.7	8.3										
20	13.0	12.3	−1.3				8.4			7.6	7.5			+6.3	+5.4						
30	13.7	13.4	3.1				7.7			7.2	7.2		6.5	6.2	5.2	5.1					
40	14.4	13.4	6.1			+7.0	6.9	+7.0	+6.4	6.8	7.0	+6.5	6.7	5.5	5.1	4.8					
50	15.1	14.4	8.1	+8.1	+7.7	6.5	6.3	7.2	6.2	6.7	6.9	6.7	7.0	5.16	5.24	4.0	+3.01	+0.14		−2.2	
60	15.9	15.3	9.0	8.1	7.39	6.14	7.0	7.4	6.25	6.6	6.3	7.0	6.3	5.24	5.43	+5.79	2.96	−0.01	+0.46	−2.0	−3.18
70	16.7	16.3	9.1	8.4	7.58	6.39	7.0	7.8	6.5	6.7	6.8	7.4	6.12	5.46	5.59	6.32	3.10	+0.05	+0.03	−1.5	−3.11
80	17.4	16.4	9.0	8.4	8.17	6.90	8.0	7.8	7.0	7.2	7.5	7.84	6.24	5.80	5.99	6.67	3.40	0.30	0.35	−1.05	2.90
90	18.1	17.4	8.9	8.4	8.94	7.64	8.8	8.0	7.7	7.28	7.6	8.38	6.37	5.46	4.74	6.97	3.87	0.74	0.49	−0.69	2.55
1800	18.7	15.3	6.3	9.4	9.62	7.64	9.35	9.0	7.81	6.60	6.9	7.84	6.73	6.24	4.8	6.32	3.87	1.33	0.43	−0.63	2.55
20	18.7	15.3	7.5	11.23	9.62	7.64	9.94	10.23	8.7	9.05	9.4	8.95	6.73	6.24	4.8	6.32	3.87	1.33	0.25	−0.14	1.56
40	19.3	15.3	8.8	11.82	10.21	8.53	10.55	10.6	10.3	9.05	10.03	9.53	8.31	6.77	5.43	7.70	4.46	2.05	0.83	+0.14	−1.56
50	19.8	15.3	7.9	12.35	9.62	8.53	10.55	10.83	10.9	9.69	10.67	10.06	8.31	7.36	5.99	7.70	5.14	2.85	1.50	0.31	−0.99
60	20.1	16.0	5.3	12.80	10.21	10.54	11.15	11.4	10.9	10.39	10.67	10.54	9.65	7.99	7.41	8.47	5.89	3.68	2.23	0.72	−0.41
70	20.1	16.4		12.80	10.97	10.54	11.7	11.4	10.9	10.39	11.21	10.54	10.21	7.99	8.18	9.2	6.65	3.68	2.23	0.72	−0.13
80	+20.3			+13.13	+11.97	+11.49	+12.2	+11.8	+12.8	+11.41	+11.63	+10.93	+10.94	+8.62	+8.9	+9.9	+7.38	+4.49	+2.96	+1.07	+0.13

TABLE OF DECIMAL VALUES OF THE MAGNETIC DECLINATION—Continued.

Year (Jan. 1).	New York, N.Y.	Hatborough, Pa.	Philadelphia, Pa.	Washington, D.C.	Cape Henry, Va.	Charleston, S.C.	Savannah, Ga.	Key West, Fla.	Havana, Cuba.	Kingston, Jamaica.	New Orleans, La.	Vera Cruz, Mexico.	Mexico, Mexico.	Acapulco, Mexico.	Panama, New Granada.	San Blas, Mexico.	San Diego, Cal.	Monterey, Cal.	San Francisco, Cal.	Cape Disappointment, Wash.	Sitka, Alaska.	Unalaska Island.
1640																						
50																						
60																						
70																						
80	+8.8	+8.5	+8.7																			
90	+8.8	+8.3	+8.3																			
1700	8.0	7.9	7.8																			
10	7.6	7.0	7.0																			
20	6.9	6.5	6.2										−1.67									
30	6.9	6.1	5.4								−3.4	−2.62	−4.7	−2.9								
40	5.2	4.7	4.6								3.7	−5.75	5.5	3.8	−7.87	−7.41						
50	4.6	3.9	3.4								4.1	6.74	6.4	4.7	7.88	7.88	−11.0	−11.4				
60	4.4	3.3	2.9							−6.2	4.7	7.63	7.1	5.4	7.84	8.28	11.3	12.0	−12.8			
70	4.29	2.9	2.4	−0.07		3.1			4.2	−6.4	5.3	8.37	7.7	6.2	7.74	8.84	11.6	12.6	13.4		−26.16	−18.98
80	4.28	2.2	2.1	+0.02	+4.44	4.1			4.5	−6.3	6.5	8.95	8.3	7.8	7.70	8.84	11.9	13.3	13.9	−18.0	27.05	19.23
90	4.30	2.03	2.98	+0.23	3.95	4.6	4.9		4.8	−6.0	6.5	9.32	8.8	7.8	7.60	8.97	12.20	13.9	14.42	18.1	27.85	19.50
1800	4.47	2.53	2.71	0.55	3.37	4.9	4.5		6.26	5.7	7.0	9.48	8.9	8.3	7.42	8.61	12.54	14.44	14.92	18.4	28.49	19.70
10	4.91	3.17	3.33	0.96	+0.22	5.1	4.14	6.9	6.12	5.4	7.5	9.42	8.9	8.08	7.20	8.97	12.88	14.95	15.78	18.7	29.11	19.82
20	4.59	3.86	4.11	1.45	+0.09	5.1	4.14	6.52	5.94	5.0	7.9	9.42	8.76	8.06	6.67	9.00	12.88	15.42	15.78	19.72	29.11	19.86
30	4.30	3.86	4.99	1.95	+0.13	4.5	3.65	6.03	5.71	4.2	8.2	9.14	8.76	8.79	6.67	9.00	12.88	15.42	15.78	19.72	29.11	19.81
40	5.59	4.57	5.89	2.47	+0.34	4.5	3.65	5.47	5.71	4.2	8.2	9.14	8.9	8.79	6.67	8.91	13.20	15.42	16.11	20.29	29.11	19.86
50	6.34	5.29	5.89	2.97	0.70	3.44	3.08	5.47	5.44	3.8	7.94	9.14	8.9	8.50	6.38	8.91	13.20	15.42	16.11	20.29	29.05	19.68
60	6.34	5.29	5.89	2.97	0.70	3.44	3.08	5.47	5.44	3.8	7.94	9.14	8.9	8.50	6.38	8.91	13.20	15.42	16.11	20.88	29.05	19.68
70	6.96	6.0	5.89	2.97	2.40	1.00	2.48	4.24	5.44	3.8	7.61	7.98	8.46	8.50	6.38	8.91	13.20	15.79	16.36	21.46	28.74	19.48
80	7.43	6.0	5.89	2.97	2.40	1.00	2.48	4.24	5.1	−3.4	7.15	7.15	7.46	−7.5	−5.79		−13.50	−16.08	−16.52	−22.00	−28.20	−19.21

It will be observed that the amount of change is by no means the same even in places not far remote from each other, as New York and Philadelphia.

In grouping together a table of the present rate of change much allowance must therefore be made for possible local peculiarities that have not been ascertained.

The following statement of the present (1878) annual change in the magnetic declination, due to the secular variation, may serve to give a general idea of the *approximate* amount of change along our immediate sea-coast. For the interior States the information is very scanty, and therefore less trustworthy, or altogether wanting.

The annual change is expressed in minutes of arc, a + sign indicating increase of westerly or decrease of easterly declination.

Locality.	Annual change.
Maine, coast of	+2
Maine, interior	+3
New Hampshire	+3½
Vermont	+5½
Massachusetts, eastern part	+2½
Massachusetts, western part	+3 to 4
Rhode Island and Connecticut	+3½
New York, Long Island	+3
New York, northern and western part	+4½
New Jersey	+3
Pennsylvania	+3½
Ohio	+2½
Tennessee, eastern part	+2½
Tennessee, western part	+2
Missouri	+2
Delaware, Maryland, and Virginia	+3
West Virginia	+3½
North Carolina, South Carolina, and Georgia	+3½
Florida, northern part	+3
Florida, southern part	+3
Alabama and Mississippi, Gulf coast of	+3
Louisiana, eastern part	+2½
Louisiana, western coast	+2
Texas, coast of	+1
Texas, southwestern part } New Mexico and Southwestern Arizona	0 (probably.)
California, coast of	−1½
Oregon, coast of	−2 to 2½
Washington Territory, coast of	−2½ to 3

The negative sign indicates an increase of easterly declination.

METHOD OF ASCERTAINING THE MAGNETIC DECLINATION OR VARIATION OF THE COMPASS.

The following chapter, on the subject of the declination of the magnetic needle, is extracted from the revised edition of the work on surveying by Dr. Charles Davies, a graduate of the Military Academy at West Point. The work itself will be a valuable acquisition to the deputy surveyor, and his attention is particularly invited to the following chapter, which sets forth the usual easy modes by which the true meridian and magnetic declination may be approximately ascertained; his attention is also called to more complete statements on the subject given in the work "A treatise on land-surveying, &c.," by Dr. W. M.

Gillespie, professor of engineering, Union College, in chapter treating of the declination of the magnetic needle. For more refined methods, he may consult Coast-Survey Report for 1875, Appendix No. 16.

METHOD OF ASCERTAINING THE VARIATION.

The best practical method of determining the true meridian of a place is by observing the north star. If this star were precisely at the point in which the axis of the earth, prolonged, pierces the heavens, then the intersection of the vertical plane passing through it and the place, with the surface of the earth, would be the true meridian. But the star being at a distance from the pole equal to 1° 30′ nearly, it performs a revolution about the pole in a circle, the polar distance of which is 1° 30′; the time of revolution is 23 hours and 56 minutes.

To the eye of an observer this star is continually in motion, and is due north but twice in 23 hours and 56 minutes; and is then said to be on the meridian. Now, when it departs from the meridian, it apparently moves east or west for 5 hours and 59 minutes, and then returns to the meridian again.

When at its greatest distance from the meridian, east or west, it is said to be at its *eastern* or *western* elongation.

The following tables show the times of its eastern and western elongations:

Time of elongation of Polaris (a Ursæ Min.), April 1, 1883, to April 1, 1884, computed for north latitude 38°, and which will serve for all latitudes from 26° to 50° north and for all dates from April, 1878, to April, 1888, with an error of less than five minutes.

[The times are reckoned from noon (astronomical time).]

EASTERN ELONGATIONS.

Day.	April.	May.	June.	July.	August.	September.
	h. m.	h. m.	h. m.	h. m.	h. m.	h. m.
1	18 37	16 39	14 37	12 39	10 37	8 36
7	18 14	16 16	14 14	12 16	10 14	8 12
13	17 50	15 52	13 50	11 52	9 50	7 48
19	17 26	15 28	13 26	11 29	9 27	7 25
25	17 03	15 05	13 03	11 05	9 03	7 01

WESTERN ELONGATIONS.

Day.	October.	November.	December.	January.	February.	March.
	h. m.	h. m.	h. m.	h. m.	h. m.	h. m.
1	18 27	16 25	14 28	12 26	10 24	8 30
7	18 04	16 02	14 04	12 02	10 00	8 06
13	17 40	15 38	13 40	11 39	9 37	7 43
19	17 17	15 15	13 17	11 15	9 13	7 19
25	16 53	14 51	12 53	10 51	8 49	6 55

The eastern elongations are put down from the beginning of April to the end of September, and the western from the beginning of October to the end of March. The time is computed from noon. The western elongations in the first case, and the eastern in the second, occurring in the day-time, cannot be used. Some of those put down are also invisible, occurring in the evening before it is dark, or after daylight in the morning.

In such case, if it be necessary to determine the meridian at that particular season of the year, let 5 hours 59 minutes be added to or subtracted from the time of greatest eastern or western elongation, and the observation be made at night when the star is on the meridian.

The following table exhibits the angle which the meridian plane makes with the vertical plane passing through the pole-star when at its greatest eastern or western elongation; such angle is called the *azimuth.*

The mean angle only is put down, being calculated for the first of July of each year.

Azimuth of Polaris (a Ursæ Min.) at elongation, 1878 *to* 1888.

(Latitude 26° to 50° north.)

	26°	28°	30°	32°	34°	36°	38°	40°	42°	44°	46°	48°	50°
	° ′	° ′	° ′	° ′	° ′	° ′	° ′	° ′	° ′	° ′	° ′	° ′	° ′
1878	1 29½	1 31¼	1 33	1 35	1 37½	1 39½	1 42¼	1 45¼	1 48½	1 52	1 56	2 00½	2 05¼
1879	29¼	30¾	32¾	34½	36¾	39¼	41¾	44¾	48	51½	55½	2 00	04¾
1880	29	30½	32¼	34¼	36½	38¾	41½	44½	47½	51	55	1 59½	04½
1881	28½	30¼	32	33¾	36	38½	41	44	47	50¾	54½	59	03¾
1882	28¼	29¾	31½	33½	35¾	38	40½	43½	46¾	50¼	54¼	58½	03½
1883	28	29½	31¼	33	35¼	37½	40¼	43	46¼	49¾	53¾	58	02¾
1884	27½	29	30¾	32¾	35	37¼	39¾	42¾	45¾	49¼	53¼	57½	02½
1885	27¼	28¾	30½	32¼	34½	36¾	39½	42¼	45½	49	52¾	57	02
1886	26¾	28¼	30	32	34	36½	39	41¾	45	48½	52¼	56½	01½
1887	26½	28	29¾	31½	33¾	36	38½	41½	44½	48	51¾	56¼	01
1888	26	27¾	29¼	31¼	33¼	35¾	38¼	41	44	47½	51½	55¾	00½

O

INSTRUCTIONS

TO THE

SURVEYORS GENERAL

OF

THE UNITED STATES,

RELATING

TO THEIR DUTIES AND TO THE FIELD OPERATIONS OF DEPUTY SURVEYORS.

PRESCRIBED, ACCORDING TO LAW, BY THE COMMISSIONER OF THE GENERAL LAND OFFICE.

WASHINGTON:
GOVERNMENT PRINTING OFFICE.
1871.

INSTRUCTIONS

TO THE

SURVEYORS GENERAL OF PUBLIC LANDS OF THE UNITED STATES.

GENERAL LAND OFFICE, *June* 1, 1864.

I.—THE SURVEYING MANUAL AND INSTRUCTIONS OF THE COMMISSIONER ARE MADE A PART OF THE SURVEYING CONTRACTS BY LAW.

By the second section of the act of Congress entitled "An act to reduce the expenses of the survey and sale of the public lands in the United States," approved May 30, 1862, it is provided, "That the printed Manual of Instructions relating to the public surveys, prepared at the General Land Office, and bearing date February twenty-second, eighteen hundred and fifty-five the instructions of the Commissioner of the General Land Office, and the special instructions of the surveyor general, when not in conflict with said printed Manual or the instructions of said Commissioner, *shall be taken and deemed a part of every contract for surveying the public lands of the United States.*"

In pursuance of law, the following instructions are prescribed for your government and that of your deputies in surveying the public lands:

II.—SURVEYS TO BE EXECUTED BY DEPUTY SURVEYORS IN PERSON.

Your attention is especially directed to the last clause of the printed form of contract furnished by this office, which stipulates "that no payment shall be made for any surveys not executed by the said deputy surveyor in his own proper person." It has been the practice of deputies to take contracts for more surveying than they could perform in person, and then employ one or more compassmen with their auxiliaries to do the work. The object of the stipulation referred to in the contract is to prevent a continuance of this practice.

Deputy surveyors are required to verify by their oath that the surveys embraced in their contracts have been executed in strict conformity with instructions, the requirements of the Surveying Manual, and the laws of the United States. The deputy cannot consistently make this oath if the work is done by separate parties in other parts of the field from where he is operating.

That there may be no misunderstanding upon this point, you are hereby instructed not to enter into contract with any one deputy for a greater amount of surveying than it may reasonably be expected he will be able to execute in one season, under his own immediate and personal direction, with *one surveying party only;* and deputy surveyors will be notified in advance that accounts for surveying done in violation of this rule will not be allowed.

When two deputies enter into joint contract for certain surveys, and *only one* of them goes into the field, if that one, with a single surveying party, executes all the work in person, his affidavit alone as surveyor, attached to the field notes, will be deemed sufficient, and no impediment to the payment of his account will result therefrom.

<small>When one Deputy does the work under a joint contract, he may verify.</small>

If two deputies, joint parties in a contract, *both* go into the field, each with a separate surveying party, the field notes must show clearly the particular surveying done by each deputy. The date and the name of the deputy will be stated at the beginning and end of the notes of every continuous part of such survey executed by him, so that it may be distinctly seen by whom each mile of line was run.

<small>Active Deputies under joint contract each to verify.</small>

The following form of affidavit is prescribed, to be attached to the field notes in cases of joint surveys, in lieu of the one heretofore used, to wit:

"I, A B, deputy surveyor, do solemnly swear that, in pursuance of a joint contract, wherein A B and C D are joint contractors with S. G., United States surveyor general for ―――――, bearing date the ―― day of ―――, 18―, I have well, faithfully, and truly, in my own proper person, and in strict conformity with the instructions furnished by the surveyor general, the Surveying Manual, and the laws of the United States, surveyed all those parts or portions of ―――――― as are represented in the foregoing field notes as having been surveyed under my direction; and I do further solemnly swear that all the corners of said surveys have been established and perpetuated in strict accordance with the Surveying Manual and printed instructions, and that the foregoing are the true and original field notes of such survey."

<small>Form of affidavit for joint surveys.</small>

The separate affidavit of each deputy, in the above form, well be attached to the field notes of joint surveys.

III.—OPERATIONS IN THE FIELD, WHEN TO COMMENCE.

The practice of anticipating the appropriations is deemed unwise and contrary to the spirit of the law. The surveys should not be commenced in advance of the year for which the means is provided by Congress, and no moneys can be used to pay for work done before they were appropriated. This must be regarded as an invariable rule to be rigidly observed in future.

The object of this restriction is to keep back the surveying operations to the legitimate period of time contemplated in the appropriations. These appropriations are made with reference to the current necessities of given years, and if allowed to be absorbed in advance, the purposes of Congress in providing stated sums annually to carry forward the public surveys would be defeated. In order to enable deputy surveyors to avail themselves of the whole season belonging to the fiscal year, however, they may be permitted to commence their operations as soon after the first day of May in each year as notice is received from this office that the appropriations have been made. You will be promptly notified, by mail or telegraph, as circumstances may determine, when the appropriations are passed, and no surveying chargeable to such appropriations must be done before receiving this notice.

IV.—CONTRACTS MUST BE APPROVED BY THE COMMISSIONER.

The first section of the act of May 30, 1862, provides that contracts for the survey of the public lands shall not become binding upon the

United States until approved by the Commissioner of the General Land Office, except in such cases as the Commissioner shall otherwise especially order.

V.—REVENUE STAMPS TO BE ATTACHED TO CONTRACTS AND BONDS.

The requirements of the internal revenue law make it necessary that *five separate stamps* be attached to the several parts of every contract and bond of a deputy surveyor, to wit:
1. To the *contract*, five-cent stamp; 2. To the *affidavit* of the deputy surveyor, five cents; 3. To the *bond*, fifty cents; 4. To the *certificate* as to the sufficiency of the bond, ten cents; 5. To the *oath* of allegiance, five cents.

Surveyors general are reminded that the sufficiency of the sureties to the bonds of deputy surveyors must be certified BY THE PROPER OFFICER OF A COURT HAVING A SEAL.

VI.—WHEN DESIRED BY SETTLERS, SURVEYS MAY BE MADE BY THE SURVEYOR GENERAL AT THEIR EXPENSE IN CERTAIN CASES.

By section 10 of an act entitled "An act to reduce the expenses of the survey and sale of the public lands in the United States," approved May 30, 1862, it is provided, "That when the settlers in any township or townships, not mineral or reserved by Government, shall desire a survey made of the same under the authority of the surveyor general of the United States, and shall file an application therefor in writing, and deposit in a proper United States depository, to the credit of the United States, a sum sufficient to pay for such survey, together with all expenses incident thereto, without cost or claim for indemnity on the United States, it shall and may be lawful for said surveyor general, under such instructions as may be given him by the Commissioner of the General Land Office, and in accordance with existing laws and instructions, to survey such township or townships, and make return thereof to the general and proper local land office: *Provided*, The townships so proposed to be surveyed are within the range of the regular progress of the public surveys embraced by existing standard lines or bases for the township and subdivisional surveys."—(Sec. 10, p. 410, vol. 12, U. S. Laws.)

Applications for surveys under this law must be made to the surveyor general in writing, upon the receipt of which he will furnish the applicant with an estimate of how much the desired survey will cost. On receiving a certificate of deposit of a United States depositary, showing that the required sum has been deposited with him in a proper manner to pay for the work, you will contract with a competent United States deputy surveyor, and have the survey made and returned in the same manner as other public surveys are.

You are especially enjoined in all cases to state explicitly in your letters furnishing estimates to applicants, that the payment of the amount required for the survey will not give the depositor any priority of claim or right to purchase the land, or in any manner affect the claim or claims of any party or parties thereto; and that, when surveyed, it will be subject to the same general laws and regulations in relation to the disposition thereof as other public lands are.

The money should be deposited to the credit of the Treasurer of the United States on account of the proper appropriations. A separate estimate is required and a separate deposit must be made for *office work* and *field work;* one to be placed to the credit of the appropriation "for compensation of the surveyor general and the clerks in his office," and the other to the credit of the appropriation "for continuing the public surveys." The depositary will issue certificates in triplicate, one of which will be transmitted to this office with the contract and bond of the deputy surveyor.

The account will be adjusted and paid in the same manner as other surveying accounts. Should the amount deposited exceed the cost of survey and all expenses incident thereto, including office work, an account setting forth the fact of such excess may be rendered by the depositor, certified by the surveyor general, and transmitted to this office with the final surveying returns, to be reported for payment.

Where a township is surveyed under the provisions of the aforesaid act, the survey must include all the *surveyable* public land in such township.

VII.—SMALL ISLANDS MAY BE SURVEYED AT THE COST OF APPLICANTS.

Many applications are received at this office for the purchase of small unsurveyed islands which were omitted when the adjacent lands were surveyed. These islands are usually of too little value to justify the Government in incurring the expense of survey; but where a party desires the survey made and is willing to pay the cost thereof in advance, upon the conditions set forth in these instructions, it may be done under the provisions of the tenth section of the act of May 30, 1862.

The party desiring the survey to be made must file a written application with the surveyor general, giving an intelligible description of the locality of the island, its distance from the main shore, the width of the narrowest channel between it and the main land, with an estimate of its area.

Upon receiving such application, made in the manner indicated, you will examine the records and data in your office, and if it appears that the island is public land and has not already been surveyed, you will furnish the applicant an estimate of the cost of surveying it, as directed under the sixth head in these instructions, stating explicitly that the depositing of the money will not in any manner affect the rights of parties in said lands, nor give any priority of claim to the depositor.

You will observe particularly that two separate deposits are to be made—one on account of the appropriation for field work, and one on account of the appropriation for office work—a separate certificate for each to be transmitted to this office with the contract and bond of the deputy surveyor.

It will be understood that these instructions relate only to isolated islands, or islands that were omitted when the public surveys were extended over the adjacent lands, and do not apply to islands falling within the regular course of current surveys, which must be included in the contracts for surveying the public lands.

As a general rule, a body of land separated from the main land by a *perpetual* natural channel may be regarded as an island for the purposes contemplated in these instructions.

VIII.—SURVEY OF SWAMP LANDS.

Contracts with deputy surveyors must of course embrace any "swamp and overflowed" lands which, in alluvial regions, are intermingled with the arable or fast lands. Over all such lands the lines of the public surveys must be extended, as the selections in such cases are made according to the character of the *smallest legal subdivision*. If the greater part of such subdivision is "swamp and overflowed," it goes to the swamp grant; if otherwise, it is excluded from such grant, and is retained by the Government.

In the survey of all lands of this mixed character, the deputies must be charged to give in their field notes a specific and full description of the land, indicating the *causes* of its being unfit for cultivation in its natural condition, with the character of the timber, shrubs, or plants growing on the tract, and the contiguity of the premises to rivers, water-courses, or lakes, naming them respectively. The swamp grant does not embrace tracts in which the inundation is casual, but only those where the overflow would totally destroy crops and prevent the raising of the same without artificial means, such as levees, draining, &c. The essentiality must be obvious to you of the requirement of full data in these respects, in order to enable the Department properly to adjust swamp and other interests.

Where the State authorities desire to have swamp lands surveyed at their expense, the same may be done in accordance with instructions on page 5 for surveys under the provisions of the tenth section of the act of May 30, 1862; but all applications for separate surveys of swamp lands must be submitted to this office, with a full report and a diagram illustrating the locality, and the approval of the Commissioner first obtained.

IX.—CERTAIN RIVERS TO BE MEANDERED ON ONE BANK ONLY.

Rivers not embraced in the class denominated "navigable" under the statute, but which are well-defined natural arteries of internal communication, and have a uniform width, will only be meandered *on one bank*. For the sake of uniformity, the surveyor will traverse the *right bank* when not impracticable; but where serious obstacles are met with, rendering it difficult to course along the right bank, he may cross to the left bank and continue the meanders as far as necessary; but all changes from one bank to the other will be made at the point of intersection of some line of the public surveys with the stream being meandered.

The subdividing deputies will be required to establish meander corners on both banks of such meanderable streams at the intersection of all section lines, and the distances across the river will be noted in the field book.

In meandering water-courses, where a distance is more than *ten chains* between stations, even chains only should be taken; but if the distance is *less* than ten chains, and it is found convenient to employ chains and links, the number of links should be a multiple of ten, thereby saving time and labor in testing the closings both in the field and in the surveyor general's office.

X.—WHAT LAKES ARE NOT TO BE MEANDERED.

Paragraph numbered three, on page 13 of the Manual, in regard to the meandering of lakes, &c., is modified as follows:

Lakes embracing an area of less than *forty acres* will not be meandered. Long, narrow or irregular lakes of larger extent, but which embrace *less than one-half* of the smallest legal subdivision, will not be meandered. Shallow lakes or bayous, likely in time to dry up or be greatly reduced by evaporation, drainage, or other cause, will not be meandered, however extensive they may be.

Deputy surveyors will be allowed pay for the distance across lakes or ponds not meandered, where they are required to continue the lines of the public surveys across them; but no offsets or lines run in triangulating will be paid for.

Where the distance across a lake or other body of water is ascertained by offsetting, it is not enough to say in the field notes "8.65 over lake and set a meander corner," but the *mode* by which the distance is ascertained must be stated and described in full.

Posts will be established by the subdividing deputy at the intersections of all the public lines with these lakes the same as if they were to be meandered.

XI.—CORNER POSTS AND CORNER STONES.

In loose or alluvial soil, section, quarter-section, or meander posts may be driven into the ground, instead of digging holes and planting them as required in the Manual; but no posts will be so driven unless, from the character of the soil, they will thereby be rendered more firm and enduring.

All corner stones fourteen inches long, or more, and less than eighteen inches in length, should be set two-thirds of their length in the ground; if more than eighteen inches long, they should be set three-quarters of their length in the ground.

XII.—QUARTER SECTION CORNERS NOT TO BE ESTABLISHED IN CERTAIN CASES.

Quarter section corners are not required to be established on the *west* boundary of the *western tier of sections* in a township, nor on the *north* boundary of the northern tier of sections in a township *south of and bordering on a standard parallel or base line.* The resurvey of township, standard, or base lines, by the deputy surveyor, for the purpose of establishing such quarter posts, is unnecessary and will not be paid for.

XIII.—POSTS IN MOUNDS.

All posts in mounds will hereafter be planted or driven into the ground to the depth of twelve inches, at the precise corner point; and the charcoal-charred stake or marked stone required in the Manual will be deposited twelve inches below the surface, against the north side of the post when the deputy is running north, and against the west side when the deputy is running west, &c.

Township mounds will be five feet in diameter at their base and two and a half feet in perpendicular height. Posts in township mounds are therefore required to be four and a half feet in length, so as to allow twelve inches to project above the mound.

Mounds at section, quarter section, and meander corners, will be four and a half feet in diameter at their base and two feet in perpendicular height, the posts being four feet in length, leaving twelve inches to project above the mound.

The planting of seeds between the pits and trenches, as directed on page 11 of the Manual, is not required.

XIV.—PITS IN LIEU OF TRENCHES.

The quadrangular trench required in connection with the construction of mounds is dispensed with. The *pits* will be continued, and should be of uniform dimensions. The pits for a township mound will be eighteen inches wide, two feet in length, and at least twelve inches deep, located six feet from the post. At section corners the pits will be eighteen inches *square*, and not less than twelve inches in depth.

At township corners common to *four* townships, the pits will be dug on the lines and lengthwise to them. On base and standard lines, where the corners are common to only *two* townships or sections, three pits only will be dug—two in line on either side of the post, and one on the line north or south of the corner, as the case may be. By this means the standard and closing corners will be readily distinguished from each other.

XV.—NOTCHING SECTION CORNER POSTS.

Posts or stones at the corners of sections in the interior of townships will have as many notches on the *south* and *east* edges as they are miles from the south and east boundaries of the township, instead of being notched on all four edges, as directed on pages 8 and 9 of the Manual.

XVI.—MARKING LINES.

In addition to the instructions under this head on page 4 of the Manual, the following requirements will be observed, to wit:

Where trees two inches or more in diameter are found, the required blazes must not be omitted.

Bushes on or near the line should be bent at right angles therewith, and receive a blow of the axe at about the usual height of blazes from the ground sufficient to leave them in a bent position, but not to prevent their growth.

On *trial* or *random* lines, when it is necessary to lop bushes, they should be bent *in the direction of the line*, to prevent mistaking random for true lines.

XVII.—BEARING TREES.

Where a tree not less than two and a half inches in diameter can be found for a bearing tree within 300 links of the corner, it should be preferred to the trench or pit. The *quadrangular trench* required on page 9 of the Manual as a substitute, where the requisite number of "bearing trees" is not found, is dispensed with, and a *pit* two feet square and not less than twelve inches deep is required in lieu thereof.

XVIII.—MODE OF CORRECTING BACK RANDOM LINES.

The manner of running random and true lines illustrated in the specimen field notes, marked "B," in the Manual, is hereby modified so as to conform to the directions on page 23; that is, the deputy, having run a random line, will correct back " by calculating a course that will run a true line back to the corner post from which the random started." For instance: instead of saying " west on a true line," &c., with an *altered* variation, say " north 89° 47′ west on a true line," &c., with *same* variation.

XIX.—ABBREVIATIONS IN THE FIELD NOTES.

The following additional abbreviations are authorized to be used in the field notes, to wit:

For quarter section corner, use "$\frac{1}{4}$ sec. cor.;" for variation, "va.;"

for 14 inches long, 12 inches wide, and 3 inches thick, in describing a corner stone, use 14 × 12 × 3, being particular to always observe the same order of length, width, and thickness.

XX.—PRESCRIBED LIMITS FOR CLOSINGS AND LENGTH OF LINES IN CERTAIN CASES.

1. Every north-and-south section line, except those terminating in the north boundary of the township, must be *eighty chains* in length.

2. The east-and-west *section lines*, except those terminating in the west boundary of the township, are to be within *one hundred links* of the actual distance established on the south boundary line of the township for the width of said tier of sections.

3. The north boundary and south boundary of any one section, except in the extreme western tier, are to be within *one hundred links* of equal length.

4. The meanders within each fractional section, or between any two meander posts, or of a pond or island in the interior of a section, must close within one chain and fifty links.

5. In running *random* township exteriors, if such random lines fall short or overrun in length, or intersect the eastern or western boundary, as the case may be, of the township, at more than *three chains and fifty links* north or south of the true corner, the lines must be *retraced*, even if found necessary to remeasure the meridional boundaries of the township.

It will be particularly observed that no changes in regard to surveying operations are made by these instructions excepting those specially stated and authorized. In every other particular the Manual and existing instructions of the Commissioner remain in full force.

Very respectfully, your obedient servant,

J. M. EDMUNDS,
Commissioner.